RHS

The LITTLE BOOK of

HAPPY
HOUSE
PLANTS

RHS The Little Book of Happy House Plants

Author: Holly Farrell

First published in Great Britain in 2018 by Mitchell Beazley, a division of
Octopus Publishing Group Ltd
Carmelite House, 50 Victoria Embankment, London EC4Y 0DZ
www.octopusbooks.co.uk

An Hachette UK Company
www.hachette.co.uk

Published in association with the Royal Horticultural Society

ISBN: 978 1 78472 424 5

A CIP record of this book is available from the British Library

Set in Gill Sans, Madurai and Amatic

Printed and bound in China

Mitchell Beazley Publisher: Alison Starling

RHS Publisher: Rae Spencer-Jones

Conceived, designed and produced by Quid Publishing
an imprint of The Quarto Group
The Old Brewery, 6 Blundell Street,
London N7 9BH, United Kingdom
T (0) 20 7700 6700 F (0)20 7700 8066
www.QuartoKnows.com

Cover design: Clare Barber

Designer: Clare Barber

Illustrations: Alyssa Peacock

RHS consultant editor: Simon Maughan

The Royal Horticultural Society is the UK's leading gardening charity
dedicated to advancing horticulture and promoting good gardening. Its charitable work includes
providing expert advice and information, training the next generation of gardeners, creating hands-on
opportunities for children to grow plants and conducting research into plants, pests and
environmental issues affecting gardeners.

For more information visit www.rhs.org.uk or call 0845 130 4646.

RHS

The LITTLE BOOK of

HAPPY
HOUSE
PLANTS

POTS OF PLANTS TO GROW INDOORS

HOLLY FARRELL

CONTENTS

Introduction...6

How to use this book...8

CHAPTER 1:

THE HOME AS A GARDEN...10

Growing inside: microclimates...12

Things to watch out for...14

House plants on display...16

CHAPTER 2:

GETTING STARTED...20

Sourcing plants...22

Choosing the right pot...24

Tools and equipment...26

Sowing seeds...28

Potting and repotting...30

Climbers and tall plants...32

CHAPTER 3:

HOW TO CREATE...34

Terrariums...36

Kokedama and string gardens...40

A succulent centrepiece...44

The hanging gardens of bathroom...48

A Christmas display...52

A child's sensory garden...56

An edible kitchen wall...60

Mindfulness with house plants...64

A windowsill cocktail garden...66

A hydroponic system of salads...68

A cleaner, greener desk space...72

Spring in a teacup...74

Creating house plants
from house plants...78

CHAPTER 4:
STAYING ALIVE...82
How to keep plants healthy...84
Watering...86
Feeding...88
Cleaning...90
Going on holiday...92
Keeping plants tidy...94
Pests...96
Diseases...98
Other potential problems...100

CHAPTER 5:
PLANT FILES...102
Key to the plant files...104
Sunny spots...106
Succulents...112
Bright spots...116
Orchids...122
Shady and humid spots...124
Bright and humid spots...128
Air plants...130
Shady and cool spots...132
Bulbs...136

Glossary...138
Further resources...140
Index...142
Credits...144

INTRODUCTION

House plants have been and always will be part of human life. There are a number of reasons why people keep plants in their homes. Some feel that being surrounded by beautiful gardens is not enough. Others wish to bring some life to their bare and grey surroundings. Keen chefs enjoy having a few fresh ingredients to hand, and people with a taste for the exotic simply wish to cultivate something weird and wonderful. For those who work from home, house plants can also bring comfort and freshness to an office space.

There have been various trends, such as Victorian hothouses, seventies macramé and Scandinavian chic, but the desire for house plants has never fully disappeared. House plants bring life to the home, and, while they make for attractive portable decorations, they are not just part of the furniture. House plants can even be part of family life, whether it's through passing a long-loved cactus down to a sibling or grandchild, or putting an aspidistra in the hall just as your parents did in your childhood home. A happy home has house plants, and a healthy home has them, too. There are proven health benefits to looking at greenery and nurturing plants, and they are also great at filtering out nasty toxins from the air, which, in an urban environment, is especially valuable.

You will discover that house plants are more than a cheap way of redecorating – they are a formative part of the home. Start with one, and you won't look back.

HOW TO USE THIS BOOK

This book provides inspiration on how to use and display plants within the home. It includes information on some of the best plants to use and guidance on how to keep them happy. There is no need to have a conservatory. Whether you have a tiny apartment or a huge house, a suntrap or a shady hall, there is a plant for all rooms and microclimates.

Chapter 1 Explores the possibilities and potential limitations of growing plants indoors: the different microclimates between and even within rooms, and inspirational ideas on how to display the plants.

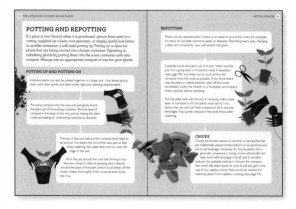

Chapter 2 Covers the fundamentals of gardening indoors, from choosing the right pot to how to look after mature plants.

Chapter 3 Provides guidance on creative planting methods, such as terrariums and kokedama, and offers some ideas for simple projects, such as a hanging display in the bathroom or a sensory garden for a child's bedroom. It also briefly explores how to use plants as air filters and as sources of mindfulness.

Chapter 4 Explains the basics of looking after house plants, from watering and fertilising to what to do about pests, diseases and going on holiday.

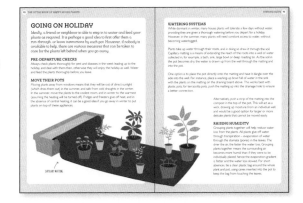

Chapter 5 Provides a guide to the most popular and the best house plants to grow, divided into groups according to type of plant (orchids, cacti and bulbs) or situation (sunny and warm spots, to shady, cool rooms).

Finally, a glossary and further resources list at the back of the book give definitions of technical terms.

CHAPTER 1

THE HOME AS A GARDEN

The different environments within a home, from a steamy bathroom to a sunny living room or a shady hallway, offer a wide range of growing possibilities – many more, in fact, than a garden. Within a single home, it is possible to grow delicate ferns and leafy tropical monsters, desert succulents and succulent dessert fruits.

There are a few potential pitfalls to growing indoors. However, if you learn what to watch out for and choose appropriately for the microclimate, you will find there is a plant for every room. Get creative with your displays: go for Scandinavian chic, recycled containers, colourful kitsch, a minimalist urban style or a classic country-house look. House plants can be adapted to suit any lifestyle and fashion choice.

GROWING INSIDE: MICROCLIMATES

Every room can accommodate at least one plant. House plants need not be restricted to windowsills – they can be put on shelves, the floor, kitchen worktops, desks or side tables, hung from the ceiling or staircases or fixed to the walls.

Each room in the house will have its own microclimate, and that can be exploited to grow a wide range of plants within a single home. These plants often are those that would not generally suit being grown in that region: for example, in a city house in Edinburgh, it is possible to grow exotic tropical plants that would have no hope of surviving the cold Scottish winters.

WHAT IS A MICROCLIMATE?

While the climate describes the general attributes of the long-term weather patterns within a country, region or city, a microclimate describes the conditions within a much smaller area, such as a room or even a single corner of that room. Different microclimates in a house can be created by variations in light and shade, humidity and warmth. For example, a steamy bathroom with south-facing, double-glazed windows and an extractor fan that doesn't work very well would have a humid, warm atmosphere. A spare bedroom with north-facing single-glazed windows and a small radiator that is set to low would have a generally cool, if not cold, shady atmosphere – unless there were guests staying, in which case the microclimate would change to being much warmer (see page 15).

A PLANT FOR EVERY SITUATION

It is always better to avoid wasting money, time and love on an unsuitable plant. Assess the various microclimates within each room and use this information to display suitable plants: lush exotic jungles in humid rooms, cacti and desert plants for sunny windowsills, ferns for shady spots. Avoid buying a plant first and putting it in a spot that simply has the wrong conditions for it. Use the Plant Files in Chapter 5 (pages 102–137) for inspiration on good plants for different situations.

THINGS TO WATCH OUT FOR

Every home will have varying temperatures through the seasons, and by and large these are things that will not affect the growth and health of house plants. Sudden and severe changes and extreme conditions, however, are what to avoid and be aware of.

DRAUGHTS

Although a plant may appear to be in a warm spot, if it is exposed to chilling and drying draughts it will suffer. Obviously, doors and windows are the main culprits, but air bricks can also create a cold breeze. Don't forget that a draught can carry a long way down a hallway.

CENTRAL HEATING

Overall, central heating can have a drying effect, and in warm rooms some plants may need to be sprayed with a light mist to retain sufficient humidity around their leaves. Avoid placing leafy plants near or above radiators as they may dry out excessively in the hot air around them, causing brown, crispy foliage.

WINDOWSILLS

On the face of it, the ideal spot for a house plant is a windowsill, but be aware, again, of extreme temperatures. Plants can be scorched easily on a sunny day, especially on leaves that are very close to, or touching, the glass. Temperature changes can also be more dramatic on a windowsill — it can get very hot when the sun is out but dramatically colder at night (especially with single glazing).

Further problems can be caused by draughty windows and frequent opening and closing of blinds or curtains, which can easily knock and damage a plant. Pets who enjoy looking out the window can also injure house plants as they seek their own space on the windowsill.

PHOTOTROPISM

This is the name given to the phenomenon whereby a plant will lean towards the strongest light source. Over time, it can lead to all the leaf growth protruding from one side of the plant, creating an uneven appearance. Rotating plants regularly will ensure even, upright growth.

DAMPNESS AND HUMIDITY

Provided suitable plants are used, damp rooms should not cause too many problems, but ensure that dead foliage and other detritus are removed promptly to avoid grey mould (*Botrytis cinerea*, see page 138) and other fungal diseases.

TEMPERATURE VARIATIONS

Plants will suffer when kept in a room that is generally kept cool but is suddenly heated, such as a guest bedroom. Similarly, plants can become damaged when left in an unheated house while the owner is on holiday (see more about this on pages 92–93). Mitigate these problems by temporarily moving plants to another location that is closer in temperature to their usual spot.

HOUSE PLANTS ON DISPLAY

Using plants as decoration allows for some really creative touches. It is a chance to express your personal style with not only the choice of plants but also the ways in which they are displayed. These suggestions are just a starting point, and websites such as Instagram and Pinterest can be fabulous sources for inspiring ideas. Generally, the more the plant is made part of the room, the better it will look.

A LUSH JUNGLE

A great thing to do in an unloved corner of a room is to group a few large, leafy plants together. Choosing plants of different heights will create interest and allow plenty of light to reach all of them. Add in some other empty pots/baskets, a rug or a piece of sculpture (it needn't be expensive; it could be driftwood from the beach).

CURATED COLLECTIONS

If you have a burgeoning collection, it is a good idea to select individual plants carefully and display them in rows in front of a painted wall. You could categorise your selection: maybe specialist plants or a particularly favoured species. Create labels that are as much a part of the display as the plants: for example, cover your pots in blackboard paint or use labels made from slate, wood or colourful plastic.

STATEMENT PLANTS

Choose a large, single plant to create a focal point in a room. It could be on a side table or on the floor, or even on its own dedicated table.

MADAGASCAR DRAGON TREE
(DRACAENA MARGINATA)

SHELFIES

Plants can be dotted around the house on shelves or bookcases. They could be displayed alone or among other treasured possessions. Putting a few different plants in the same style of pot is an easy trick to create unity of design. Alternatively, group potted plants on a shelf in different-shaped containers that are of the same colour.

KIDS AND KITSCH

Get children involved in planting a little landscape for their bedrooms – perhaps incorporating plastic toys, such as dinosaurs in a mini-jungle. Fake birds, butterflies and bees dotted around evergreen foliage can add colour.

KITCHEN GARDEN

Bring the garden into the kitchen with herbs, salads, edible flowers and microgreens, which you can then have immediately to hand for creating fresh-tasting, flavourful dishes. Seed merchants are always introducing new vegetable and fruit varieties suitable for container growing, and there's no reason why those containers cannot be inside.

SEASONAL DISPLAYS

Ideal for rooms that are in need of a bit of cheer all year round, or to brighten up a desk space, a container of mixed seasonal plants can be created simply and affordably using plants widely available at garden centres and supermarkets.

HANGING GARDENS

Plants don't have to always grow up — they can also trail down. This is a particularly great way to introduce greenery to smaller rooms without taking up too much space. Wall-mounted brackets for pots are great for a hallway. You can also try using suspended containers to hang plants over banisters. Hanging baskets can be used in the kitchen for edibles, such as strawberries, tomatoes or nasturtiums, or elsewhere in the house for permanent features of trailing foliage plants. You can even find hanging terrariums.

RECYCLED CHIC

Create individual containers that are also environmentally friendly by recycling old pots — collect a few matching ones for different plants, build little crates from bits of reclaimed wood, or paint or cover old pots and trays.

CHAPTER 2

GETTING STARTED

With house plants, as with all gardening, the key to success is to start small. It is very easy to get carried away in garden centres and nurseries, and on the Internet. Try just a couple to begin with, rather than filling the entire house with plants, and see how you get on with those before slowly expanding and accumulating a collection.

Remember that all of these plants will take time to look after, and take up space. However, getting started with house plants is very easy. If you have the necessary space and funds, gradually establishing a collection is simple.

This chapter will help you on your way. It details some of the ways to get hold of good plants, what is needed to care for them (very little that isn't already in a kitchen drawer) and a few basic techniques: for example, sowing seeds, potting and repotting plants, and supporting climbers.

SOURCING PLANTS

In recent years, there has been something of a revival in the trend for house plants, and the mainstream suppliers, such as garden centres, are slowly introducing more varied and interesting stock where before they may have sold only a few spider plants. These can be a good place to go for the more basic house plants, which are no less beautiful, such as *Phalaenopsis* orchids, various leafy palms and the low-maintenance yuccas.

Garden centres usually have a collection of small succulents among their offerings. You will often find a larger selection of house plants through online garden suppliers. If you prefer to buy offline, shops branded as 'plant centres' (such as those belonging to the RHS) usually have more of a focus on plants than highstreet 'garden centres'.

SPECIALIST NURSERIES

If you are looking for something in particular, such as a certain carnivorous plant or something for a terrarium, specialist nurseries will offer far more varied and unusual options, and can also offer advice on purchasing the correct plant. An online search easily reveals some good options, but be sure that the company has at least a no-quibbles return policy and preferably a guarantee on its plants. You will find a good source of prepotted terrariums on the Internet via specialist sites or online craft markets.

BUDGET OPTIONS

There are cheaper ways to get hold of plants. Seek out local plant sales for some bargains, or join a local gardening club, where you can meet fellow growers who are likely to have a few house plants from which they will happily take cuttings or seeds. Buying bare-root plants, i.e. plants not in a container, can be an option for woody and perennial species, and is generally cheaper than buying potted plants.

Family members and friends may have plants they no longer want, or may be able to supply cuttings. Many house plants will grow easily, if not quickly, from cuttings. Succulents also produce 'baby' plants, known as pups, that can be severed from the main plant and potted to grow into a new mature plant. See pages 78–81 for more information. The RHS website also has details on how to propagate various house plant species.

PLANTS FROM PIPS

Fruit scraps and pips are a source of free house plants – try planting a carrot top or a pineapple crown, or growing an avocado from the stone. See the further resources on page 140 for guides to these activities, which are especially great to do with children.

QUARANTINE

It is always best to keep new plants in isolation for a few days before introducing them to the rest of your collection, just in case there are any pests or diseases that weren't immediately obvious. This way, you will avoid spreading trouble unnecessarily.

CHOOSING THE RIGHT POT

When it comes to choosing the correct pot for your house plant, there are a couple of basic things to consider. The pot should be large enough to hold the plant, taking into account some growth. Otherwise, the plant can be either restricted in size or repotted into a larger container at a later date. Whatever pot you choose, it must also accommodate the need for watering.

The aesthetics, however, is entirely down to personal taste and budget. It's a good idea to make sure the style and colour of the pot will not only suit the room but also suit the plant.

FREESTYLE POTS

With the resurgence of the house plant's popularity, designers and homeware shops are offering an increased range of pots to choose from, but home-made options are unique and could cost you a lot less. Try jazzing up a basic pot by painting it with blackboard paint, which you could then decorate with chalk, or by wrapping it in a piece of fabric or strip of silver birch bark.

Alternatively, think 'outside the pot' and use containers that might not be conventionally used as plant pots. You could, for example, try one of the following:
- recycled kitchen tins and cans
- old stereo speakers
- disused chairs with the upholstery taken out of the seat
- unwanted shoes – think wellies, or even stilettos!

WATERING AND DRAINAGE

There are two options for potting a house plant: either the plant goes directly into a closed pot – the container that will be on display – or it is kept in a plastic pot with drainage holes that is then disguised by a more attractive outer pot (which is usually watertight).

For easy, mess-free watering, the latter option is best, and there is less risk of over-watering, provided excess water is not allowed to pool in the base of the outer pot. Closed pots have no drainage holes and need more careful watering to ensure the compost does not become too sodden.

ORCHID POTS

Many garden centres and retailers sell orchid pots: colourful, attractive outer pots that can hold an orchid (usually *Phalaenopsis*) in a clear plastic pot. The roots of orchids, as well as the leaves, contain chlorophyll and will grow up towards the light to get the required nutrients. This can look messy, depending on your point of view, and can make the plant unstable in the pot. A clear pot allows light to get into the pot so the roots don't have to climb out in search of light.

It is ideal, though not necessary, to keep an orchid in a clear glass or plastic pot with drainage holes, as this will mean most of the roots will stay inside the pot. It's also useful for checking how moist the soil is inside the pot.

TOOLS AND EQUIPMENT

These days, as is the case for most hobbies, there is an array of fancy gadgets to tempt house plant enthusiasts. However, keeping house plants really doesn't require a lot of equipment, and most of what you will need can be found in a well-equipped kitchen.

POTS AND CONTAINERS

While many house plants will be happy for quite a while, sometimes years, in the pot in which they were bought, there will usually come a point when a plant should be repotted into a larger container (see page 31).

This could be a cheap and cheerful recycled food container (though always put drainage holes in the bottom where possible) or a more expensive ceramic, terracotta or glass pot. Cheaper plastic pots can be hidden within other containers, for practical and aesthetic reasons; these can make for a more creative display and are a means of containing any drips or compost leaking from drainage holes. Otherwise, to protect your surfaces, it is a good idea to rest the pot on some form of saucer or tray.

To create indoor hanging gardens, all sorts of designs from seventies-style macramé baskets to sleek, modern ceramics are available. Again, check that nothing is going to drip onto the floor and that the wires and hooks are strong enough to take the weight (a plant that has just been watered will be heavy). High-tech options, such as hydroponic systems, usually come with everything included.

COMPOST

For many plants, a basic multipurpose compost will work, but cacti and succulents will need a sandier, more free-draining variety, and orchids prefer a bark/moss mix. Check the Plant Files (pages 102–137) for the perfect compost for each plant. Don't use garden soil, or any home-made compost or rotted manure, as these could carry pathogens that might multiply freely when indoors.

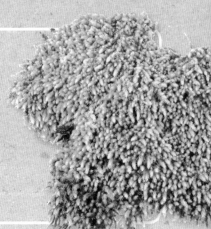

WATERING CAN

There's no need to invest in a watering can, as a bottle or glass will do the job. However, a watering can is an attractive addition to a tool collection. House plant cans tend to have long narrow spouts that pour neatly into the pot and can easily reach the base of the plant, even if it is in an inaccessible spot such as a high shelf.

USEFUL TOOLS

Other useful tools include:
- a soft cloth and paintbrush for cleaning
- sharp scissors or secateurs for pruning
- a sharp knife (such as a bread knife) and trowel for potting and repotting
- a sieve for removing large bits from multipurpose compost
- a thermometer (ideally one that records the maximum and minimum temperatures) for monitoring more temperamental plants
- purpose-made soft horticultural twine for tying in plants.

SOWING SEEDS

Growing from seed is often cheaper than buying plants and, although it may take a little more effort, can offer greater satisfaction. The process is relatively straightforward, and the large number of seeds that come in a packet (relative to the number of plants actually required) allows for any mistakes made along the way.

GROWING ANNUALS

Examples of annuals that could be grown as house plants include pot marigolds (*Calendula officinalis*), cigar plant (*Cuphea ignea*) and various vegetables, such as salad leaves, tomatoes and chilli peppers. Most dwarf varieties of garden annuals (and biennials, which flower in their second year) will be suitable for sowing and growing indoors – or even the standard-sized varieties, if given sufficient space.

GROWING RARE PLANTS FROM SEED

Seeds are much easier to store and transport, and so there is a wider availability of exotic and rare species and cultivars in seed than as grown plants. Sowing unusual perennials, shrubs, climbers and even small trees this way can be relatively cheap and will result in a unique collection of house plants. However, this process will likely involve a long-term investment of your time and effort, as many of these plants will be slow to grow.

ANNUALS AND PERENNIALS

Annual plants are those that will grow from a seed and, within a single year or growing season, flower to make more seeds before dying. Perennials are plants that come back year after year. They can be short- or long-lived; for instance, herbaceous perennials have foliage that dies back every autumn and grows afresh in spring.

SEED-SOWING BASICS

Before sowing, check the seed packet or the information sheet provided by the supplier, as this should include the information about when and how to sow. As a general rule, a seed is sown at a depth equal to twice its size. Thus, a small seed is sown with only a very thin covering and a larger seed is sown a little deeper.

Use a proprietary seed-sowing compost or sieved multipurpose compost – the aim is to have only fine particles. Fill the pot or tray evenly, tapping down to ensure it is settled, and water thoroughly before sowing the seeds. Seeds can be covered with more compost or, for fine seeds, vermiculite, which is available in small bags from good garden centres and other garden suppliers (remember to first check the supplier's instructions to see whether the seed needs light or darkness to germinate).

To ensure a good result, multiple seeds can be sown in a tray and then the best seedlings potted out once they are big enough.

Pots and trays can be covered with a clear plastic lid, a sheet of glass or, if extra heat is required to speed up germination, placed in a heated propagator or a warm place. Once the seedlings have emerged, remove the coverings to allow for good air circulation.

POTTING AND REPOTTING

If a plant is root-bound when it is purchased, grown from seed or a cutting, supplied as a bare-root specimen, or simply would look better in another container, it will need potting up. Potting on is done for plants that are being moved into a larger container. Repotting is refreshing plants by putting them into the same container with new compost. Always use an appropriate compost or mix for your plants.

POTTING UP AND POTTING ON

Individual plants can also be potted together in a larger pot – but always group them with other plants that have similar light and watering requirements.

Put some compost into the new pot and gently knock the plant out of its existing container. Test the level of compost in the base of the new pot by resting the plant inside and adding or subtracting compost as required.

The top of the root ball and the compost level need to be around 1cm below the rim of the new pot, so that when watering, the water does not run over the edge of the pot.

Fill in the pot around the root ball, firming it into the new compost without pressing down directly around the base of the plant (which could break off the roots). Water thoroughly. If the compost level drops, top it up.

REPOTTING

Plants can be repotted even if there is no need to prune the roots; for example, to check for possible soil-borne pests or diseases. Repotting every year, changing a little old compost for new, will refresh the plant.

Carefully knock the plant out of its pot. Wash out the pot if it is going back in. Prune the roots if necessary (see page 94), and shake out as much of the old compost from the roots as possible. If you think there may be pests or weeds present, wash off the roots completely under the shower or a hosepipe, and inspect them carefully before repotting.

Put the plant back into the pot. If necessary, add a base layer of compost to lift the plant's root ball to 1cm below the rim, and use fresh compost to fill in around the edges. Top up the compost if the level drops after watering.

CROCKS

Crocks are broken pieces of ceramic or terracotta that are traditionally placed at the bottom of an earthenware pot to aid drainage. However, for house plants, this is generally unnecessary. Using crocks will actually not help much with drainage, if at all, and it certainly reduces the available volume in the pot for compost, into which the plant needs to root. It will also get in the way of any capillary action that would be needed for watering plants from capillary matting (see page 93).

CLIMBERS AND TALL PLANTS:
SUPPORTS AND TRAINING

Growing a climbing plant is a great way to fill your house with foliage without taking up a lot of floor space, as it grows from a single pot. They can be trained over archways, around windows, up a stairwell or around a conservatory. Provided they get the light and conditions they need, they can adapt to most situations.

TRAINING A CLIMBING PLANT

It is always easier to put in the support system for a climber before the plant reaches the point at which it will need it, rather than trying to fiddle around supporting it after it has started to grow. The easiest way to create a training system is to use strong wires, stretched taught between eyelet screws and attached to a wall, staircase or the wooden trim of a conservatory.

If the plant is naturally twining, it will wind itself around the wire, and little intervention will be needed other than to tuck in a wayward stem here and there. Others will need regular tying in. How often you will need to do so depends on the plant, but, in general, ties should be placed at intervals so that the stem is not bowing significantly below the wire.

Use soft horticultural twine to tie in the stems using a figure-of-eight tie. Loop the twine around the stem, cross over the ends and loop around the wire, always tying off against the wire rather than the stem. Avoid tying the twine too tight; you should allow a little space for the stem to grow in thickness. Check ties regularly and replace them as necessary.

Once a climbing plant reaches the end of the support system (e.g. it has grown all the way over an archway or doorway), the growing tips will need regular pruning to stop it growing any further.

Less vigorous climbers can also be trained over a trellis, obelisk or other wire structure that is secured within their pot. Try wiring two hanging baskets together and placing them in the top of a large pot. Train the plant (ivy, perhaps) around the structure to create a dome shape.

SUPPORTS FOR TALL PLANTS

Many tall palms and other plants will happily grow up without the need for supports, but others will need something to lean on. A bamboo cane is the cheapest and easiest option, and some plants will come supplied with a mossy pole in the pot (such as *Monstera deliciosa*, Swiss cheese plant), into which the plant can root and thereby pull itself up. Alternatively, a small metal or wooden obelisk could be put in the pot for the plant to grow up and through.

CHAPTER 3

HOW TO CREATE

In this chapter, the focus is on specific growing styles and methods, such as terrariums, kokedama, vertical planting and hydroponics (growing without soil). There is more information on why and how plants can be used as air filters, and ideas for how to group plants together to create displays for specific rooms, such as 'the hanging gardens of bathroom', or for particular purposes, such as a sensory garden for children or a windowsill cocktail garden. These displays can be temporary or seasonal, for use at Christmas or springtime, for example, because house plants can ring the changes as much as outdoor gardens.

TERRARIUMS

Terrariums could possibly be the most fascinating type of indoor planting. Beautiful, magical and an ideal means of observing a number of scientific principles (or teaching them – they are great for children), these tiny worlds are straightforward to create.

CONTAINER CHOICE

A terrarium is by its very nature a closed system – all the air and water is recycled – so the chosen container should have no drainage holes and be sealable. It should also be made of glass – preferably clear glass so enough light can penetrate the plants for photosynthesis.

Examples of suitable terrarium containers include preserving jars and bottles, such as those made by Kilner. There are also specialised cases (such as miniature greenhouses) and containers available to buy. They can be as small as a test tube or as large as a demijohn. Consider the width of the neck of the container, too: it must be wide enough to be able to put in the gravel, compost and plants. Be sure to clean and dry your chosen container thoroughly before use.

WHAT TO PLANT

The best plants for terrariums are those that have evolved in and adapted to living in warm, humid, slightly shady conditions, such as ferns and most tropical leafy plants. For example, *Ficus pumila* (creeping fig), species of *Fittonia* and miniature palms, such as *Howea,* will all work well in a terrarium.

Buy the plants as small as possible. Some garden centres and nurseries now sell miniature plants suitable for terrariums, or you could look online for some. Alternatively, clumps could be divided from larger plants. If planting more than one variety in a single container, consider how all the different plants will look when together.

FITTONIA

PLANTING LAYERS

Terrariums are at their most attractive when the distinct planting layers can be easily seen through the side of the container, so make them quite thick.

The bottom third of the container is taken up with the planting and drainage layers, leaving the rest for the plants' stem and leaf growth. Everything in the base of the terrarium should be sterile (use shop-bought rather than home-made garden compost), to avoid importing pathogens that would happily multiply in the warm, humid conditions. A funnel or folded paper chute can help to spread everything evenly over the base.

METHOD

At the bottom goes a layer of gravel. It could be brightly coloured or made from glass instead of stone. Small bags of gravel can be purchased from garden centres or aquatic suppliers.

On top of the gravel, add a layer of activated charcoal. This is widely available online and from anywhere that sells fish and fish tanks, as it's used to purify water. It will serve the same purpose in the terrarium, helping to keep bacteria to a minimum.

Ideally, use seed and potting compost for the final layer because this is finer and contains fewer nutrients, though sieved multipurpose compost would also suffice if there is nothing else available. Again, make sure it is sterile and has not been sitting in a damp, forgotten corner for a year. As with the other layers, make the compost layer quite thick to allow for plenty of rooting space for the plants.

Planting your display can be tricky and, depending on the width of the vessel's neck, can require the help of some chopsticks or tweezers.

First, use a stick or skewer to make a hole in the compost. Unpot the plant and shake or wash off all the potting compost from the roots – this will make it smaller and easier to squeeze into the container.

Manoeuvre the roots into the hole, then fill in and firm the plant in place. It may help to improvise some tools by fixing a cork or other swab-like attachment to the end of a stick.

Repeat the process for as many plants as desired, and perhaps finish by adding some gravel or moss over the surface.

For a child's terrarium, tiny plastic toys, such as dinosaurs or jungle animals, are a nice touch.

MAINTENANCE

Use a spray bottle to mist the plants and the compost until the entire surface is saturated. This can also help to wash down any compost that is stuck to the sides of the vessel; otherwise, a bit of cotton wool or cloth fixed to a stick can be used to wipe the vessel clean. Finally, seal the container. It may need opening up in the first week or two for another spray but, once settled, will no longer need any watering.

KOKEDAMA AND STRING GARDENS

The Japanese art of kokedama (literally meaning 'moss ball') involves no pots at all. Instead, plants grow from a ball of clay and moss formed around their roots, which can then be placed on a surface or suspended from the ceiling. This technique looks most effective when used on groups of the same plant – a display style called a 'string garden'.

WHAT TO PLANT

Almost any plant can be planted in a kokedama, but some work better than others. For temporary, easy-to-create displays, use flowering bulbs such as snowdrops and species of *Muscari*. More permanent plantings could be made from most perennials (although avoid those with large, thin leaves that wilt easily) and traditional house plants. Many string gardens are made useing tree seedlings, which are ideal, as they are slow-growing.

KOKEDAMA FROM BULBS

Temporary plantings of bulbs (bare of any soil) need only be wrapped in a good-sized ball of moss and string, then misted thoroughly before hanging.

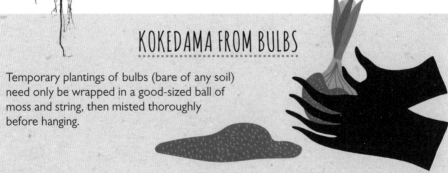

METHOD

Take the plant out of its pot and carefully put to one side. Fill the pot with two-thirds peat moss and one-third akadama (a specialist bonsai soil, available online).

Then, tip the mixture into a bowl and mix thoroughly with enough water to stick it together.

Crumble away the potting compost from the plant's roots, then mould the kokedama mix around the roots, to form a ball.

Wrap the ball tightly in sphagnum moss (available in bags from garden centres and online) so that none of the soil mix is visible.

Use string to wrap the whole thing in a criss-cross fashion. If the plant is to be hung up, add another long loop of string, carefully secured to the plant, so that the plant's stem is at the top of the ball when suspended.

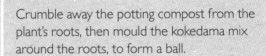

MAINTENANCE

Check if a kokedama plant needs water by weighing it – the lighter it feels, the less water it contains. To water, take the plant down and submerge in a bucket of water for an hour, remove and let it finish dripping (hang it over the bath or sink) before returning it to its usual spot. A half measure of liquid fertiliser can be added to the water in spring and summer.

A SUCCULENT CENTREPIECE

Succulents have naturally geometric shapes that lend themselves so well to being displayed in a configuration with a repeating pattern. This makes a great low-maintenance centrepiece for a dining or kitchen table. The resulting display is fascinating when viewed as a whole, but it's also entirely possible dinner guests will get lost in admiring the intricate detail of the individual plants.

CHOOSING A CONTAINER

Choose a shallow dish for the container – it need not have drainage holes, but take care not to overwater the plants.

A circular dish is ideal, but rectangular and square vessels also work well, especially if they have sharp rather than rounded corners, which will give the display a very modern look.

WHAT TO PLANT

Providing they are small (i.e. supplied in miniature pots), any succulents or cacti would be suitable for this centrepiece.

ECHEVERIA

SEMPERVIVUM

At its simplest and best, this container could be filled with alternating diagonal stripes of two different species of houseleeks (*Sempervivum*) or *Echeveria*. Some of the latter have such glaucous tones that would work particularly well against other darker and greener species, such as *E. elegans* and *E.* 'Black Prince'.

SEDUM

The aim is to have several of each plant arranged in a pattern that best sets off their individual colouring, shapes and heights, while still achieving a pleasing overall display.

METHOD

Both succulents and cacti prefer well-drained soil, so use a half-and-half mix of multipurpose compost and grit (horticultural-grade fine gravel, available from garden centres).

Before planting, lay the plants out to check the spacing – for the best effect, there should be no visible bare compost.

Water carefully so as not to oversaturate the compost.

MAINTENANCE

Keep the planter in a sunny position, and water as required, aiming to get the spout of the watering can directly over the compost rather than splashing over the leaves, which can rot if left wet in these conditions.

In the summer months, a half-strength diluted liquid fertiliser will also be of benefit to your plants.

Pick or cut off any shrivelled, dead or rotting leaves as necessary – a pair of tweezers is a useful tool for this.

Any baby plants produced can be teased out, cutting away some root as well as the tiny rosette, and planted in their own pots. Replant the whole container after a year or so, in springtime, to refresh it.

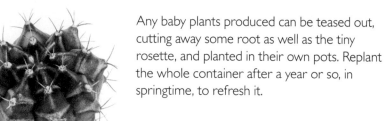

THE HANGING GARDENS OF BATHROOM

Bathrooms, with their warm, humid atmosphere, make an ideal place to keep a house plant. It will help to remove some of the moisture in the air and subsequently need less frequent watering – a win-win situation! However, there can often be limited surface and floor space. The solution is to hang the plants from the walls or ceiling.

CHOOSING A CONTAINER

The 1970s trend for macramé (knotted string) pot holders has recently been revived, but there are also plenty of other more minimalist designs of hanging pots available that can attach to walls or ceilings. Outdoor hanging baskets, when lined sufficiently, are an inexpensive option that can hold several specimens in one container.

WHAT TO PLANT

Refer to the Plant Files (pages 102–137) for examples of plants that will thrive in a bathroom's microclimate – essentially all those that originate from jungle habitats. Avoid any spiky or scratchy plants, for obvious reasons!

PLANTING

As with standing pots, hanging containers can be either planted into directly, or used to house a plant that's in a plastic pot. Take into account the weight of the plant and compost when wet, and avoid using heavy pots. Likewise, make sure that the wires or string and wall/ceiling fittings are up to the job and can take the strain.

Repetition and symmetry always look good, so consider having two identical planters and plants, such as spider plants (*Chlorophytum comosum*) hanging either side of a window.

A NATURAL SCREEN

Use several long trailing plants, such as species of ivy (*Hedera*) or hearts on a string (*Ceropegia woodii*), suspended in a line at the same height to create a screen, perhaps in place of a window blind.

A HANGING FOREST

Suspend a collection of plants from the ceiling. Hang them close together but at different heights, considering the heights and trailing habits of each plant, to display them to their best advantage.

HEDERA COLCHICA 'SULPHUR HEART'

MAINTENANCE

It is usually easier to leave a hanging plant where it is for watering, but if taking it down, stand the pot on an upturned bucket or put it on the edge of a work surface so that trailing stems are not broken by being pushed horizontally.

Water thoroughly as usual, but pour on very slowly with plenty of pauses, to allow the water to seep in and avoid potential overflow onto the floor.

A CHRISTMAS DISPLAY

House plants come into their own in the winter season, when they bring real cheer and life to indoors compared with an often drab and dreary world outside. By putting a few carefully selected seasonal plants together in a large container, a stylish and seasonal display can be created very easily. How much glitter and tinsel to add is entirely down to personal taste!

AN EVERGREEN ARRANGEMENT

The dark green tones of conifers and ivy show that their leaves are full of chlorophyll, and they are used to relatively shady positions, making them ideal for an indoor planter in winter. They will happily last through two or three months, including over the Christmas period, but will appreciate being potted up and moved outside in spring to recuperate (bring them back in again the following winter to repeat this temporary display).

WHAT TO PLANT

Try using miniature or young conifer trees – those of a classic Christmas-tree shape are commonly sold relatively cheaply in supermarkets and garden centres in winter as baby Christmas trees – and young ivy (*Hedera helix*) plants.

BABY
CONIFER

IVY

Plant up a large bowl, putting one or more (odd numbers work best aesthetically) trees in the centre and filling around the edge and underneath with ivy plants.

ROSEMARY

An alternative would be to use a standard (lollipop-shaped) bay (*Laurus nobilis*), olive (*Olea europaea*) or rosemary (*Rosmarinus officinalis*) tree as the centrepiece, providing it can be displayed in a bright spot. Use multipurpose compost and water as required so that the compost does not dry out.

OLIVE

BAY

USING FORCED BULBS

A more colourful temporary display can be created using forced bulbs, though the timing can be quite varied, and it's best not to rely on them being in bloom for a particular date.

Amaryllis (*Hippeastrum*) and paperwhite daffodils (*Narcissus*) are the two most commonly forced bulbs for mid-winter and are widely available either as dry pre-treated bulbs or ready-potted and growing. Both will have been subjected to a cold spell, and bringing them into a warm house then tricks the bulb into thinking it is spring and time to flower.

Pot up dry bulbs into a multipurpose compost – putting in as many as will fit in a single layer for the best display, as they will be split and replanted after flowering – and water as required.

Keep in the brightest, sunniest spot possible, although they can be moved once flowering to a better position. The warmer the room, the faster the flowers will go over. See also pages 74 and 136 for more ideas and advice on using bulbs.

A CHILD'S SENSORY GARDEN

A house plant or two is a great addition to a child's bedroom, but why not take it a step further and create a miniature garden? It's an ideal project to do together, and giving a child (of almost any age) some autonomy over plant choice and decorations means that they will engage with it that much more.

The child's age will, to some extent, influence the type of garden that is best to create – for example, a display full of prickly cacti is probably not the best choice for toddlers. Encourage children to look at the colours and feel the different shapes and textures of plants, and to take some responsibility for looking after them.

The following pages have some ideas for plant displays that will work well together and have particularly sensory properties. As long as the plants all have similar light, heat and watering requirements, it's possible to let their creativity run riot.

The varied forms and low-maintenance nature of succulents make them ideal starter plants for children.

A HOT, SANDY DESERT

For the cowboy fans in your life, create a little desert landscape in a wide, shallow container.

Plant miniature succulents, such as money tree (*Crassula ovata*), aloes (*Aloe vera* and other species) and living stones (*Lithops*). For older children, perhaps add some differently shaped cacti.

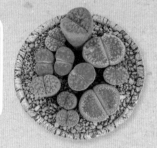

Leave some space between the plants or around the edge, and cover the compost surface with a layer of sand and/or glass pebbles or gravel, which will introduce different textures.

This display could be the basis for some imaginary playtime activity with desert animals, or for acting out a Hollywood western.

A JUNGLE OF TEXTURES

A large, deep and stable pot housing some plants of different heights and textures can bring a jungle feel to the corner of a room.

Planting everything in one large pot, rather than having a collection of smaller ones, means it is less likely the pot will get knocked over (intrepid explorers may want to hide in this new 'jungle').

ANTHURIUM

The tree-like ornamental fig (*Ficus*) can look effective in a jungle display and will leave enough root space for other plants to grow. *Ctenanthe* work well with other leafy plants, such as the colourful croton (*Codiaeum*) or banner plant (*Anthurium*), with its weird waxy flowers.

Underplanting *Fittonia*, which has brightly veined leaves, completes the jungle layers. Enlist little hands to help mist and clean the leaves regularly.

Jungle plants are
ideal for budding
naturalists
and explorers.

AN EDIBLE KITCHEN WALL

Even a kitchen with no windowsills or spare surface space can have some fresh herbs, or even fruits and vegetables growing in it, thanks to innovations in vertical growing. A vertical wall of produce is practical – being easily at hand to use at its maximum freshness – as well as beautiful.

CHOOSING A CONTAINER

The container options for wall gardens basically fall into the following categories:
- fixed structures that mount to the wall and can hold various pots
- actual pots and troughs that can be fixed directly to the wall
- more flexible, modular systems of material planting pockets.

The only caveat is to ensure that the wall behind will be sufficiently protected from any water or damp (usually the product you buy will include this protection) and that both the wall and the fixings are strong enough to take the weight of the fully watered, fully grown plant (or plants) and the compost.

WHAT TO PLANT

Leafy and trailing plants are best for covering containers and creating a green wall appearance, but if the containers are a feature, many culinary plants can be used.

Use annual and bushy herbs such as basil, parsley, thyme, mint, lemon balm, coriander, and chamomile. Shrubby upright herbs, such as rosemary and sage, will eventually outgrow small containers and won't regrow new leaves quickly, but young plants can be used for a short time.

Also worth considering are dwarf and tumbling tomatoes (those bred for growing in windowsill pots and hanging baskets), such as 'Tumbling Tom Red' and 'Hundreds and Thousands'.

Other edible favourites to try are dwarf cucumbers, cucamelons (grape-sized melons that grow on an attractive, scrambling vine and taste like cucumbers), strawberries, salad leaves, nasturtiums, radishes and spring onions.

Fabric planting pouches can bring greenery and fresh produce to the smallest of spaces.

If you have bought a ready-made planter, follow the instructions on the product. If you wish to give it a more personal feel, use a little DIY skill to mount the pockets or planters with a wooden frame surround. This can make an even more decorative feature (a piece of living art).

Paint your frame or pots to make them look more attractive in your kitchen. You may wish to paint them with blackboard paint to add plant labels (useful for identifying plants when you are cooking).

Any multipurpose compost can be used. Crops can be grown directly from seed in the wall or purchased as young plants.

MAINTENANCE

It is possible to add an automatic watering system, such as drip-line irrigation. This could be worth considering for large-scale wall plantings, as the small pockets of compost can dry out easily. In most cases, however, hand watering is just as practical and cheaper.

MINDFULNESS WITH HOUSE PLANTS

Mindfulness, the practice of training the mind to focus on being aware of one's surroundings to quieten the rest of the chatter in the brain, can be as simple as concentrating on the breath, but can also involve bringing the attention to an object or repetitive activity.

As plants and gardening are already well known to bring a sense of peace and calm, combining the two is a logical choice, and very easy to do when using house plants, leading to happy house plants and a happy mind.

The aim is to have something to completely focus the attention and senses on, for 5 to 10 minutes a day. It is better to use a single plant, rather than a collection, as in this way concentration can be more readily focussed. It could be a high-maintenance orchid, or a similar tropical plant, which needs time spent on it; for example, misting and cleaning the leaves every day. Alternatively, it could be a plant that has elements that are particularly stimulating to the senses, such as fragrant flowers or tactile leaves, or one that is simply captivating to look at.

HOW TO BE MINDFUL

If carrying out maintenance, concentrate entirely on the sensations: for example, the action of squeezing the misting bottle handle, the feel of some of the water falling on the hand and the look of the water as it falls through the light and onto the plant. If sitting in contemplation of a plant, focus the attention on it and really look, smell or feel the plant, appreciating every nuance.

It is perfectly natural for the attention to wander during these exercises, but bringing it back to the task at hand is all part of training the mind to focus.

WHAT TO PLANT

Tactile plants, such as air plant (*Tillandsia argentea*), Delta maidenhair fern (*Adiantum raddianum*), Boston fern (*Nephrolepis exaltata*) and African violet (*Saintpaulia*).

Fragrant plants, such as lemon grass (*Cymbopogon citratus*), lemon verbena (*Aloysia citrodora*), citrus trees (*Citrus*), jasmine (*Jasminum*), lilies (*Lilium*) and *Pelargonium*.

AIR PLANT

Visually interesting and/or detailed plants, such as auriculas (*Primula auricula*), Cape primrose (*Streptocarpus*), cacti, bromeliads (*Nidularium, Neoregelia*), *Solenostemon* and *Fittonia*.

AFRICAN
VIOLET

JASMINE

A WINDOWSILL COCKTAIL GARDEN

Kitchen windowsills or sunny spots on worktops and dining tables are the ideal place for edible house plants, especially when growing crops that can be used as soon as they are picked. Culinary herbs are an obvious choice, but for something a little different, grow garnishes and flavourings for a home-grown cocktail party.

THE BOTANICALS COLLECTION

For gin cocktails, use herbs with flavours that will complement the botanicals of the spirit. Robust and punchy-flavoured plants, such as the Greek lemon basil (*Ocimum basilicum*) or lemon thyme (*Thymus citriodorus*), lemon verbena (*Aloysia citrodora*) and rose-scented pelargonium (*Pelargonium* 'Attar of Roses' is a good choice), will all grow well on a sunny windowsill.

MINT

ALPINE STRAWBERRY

THE PIMM'S GARNISH COLLECTION

If you have the space, try planting these together in one large planter. Dwarf cucumber plants (varieties suitable for pots or labelled as 'dwarf') or cucamelons can climb up supports or trail over the edge. Borage will grow tall – pinch out the growing tips of young plants to create a bushy rather than tall plant – and alpine strawberries will cover the rest of the pot to complete the garnish.

MUDDLING HERBS

For a mojito or other long drink, mint is hard to beat. Virtually indestructible, it is easy to propagate by putting a stem in water until it sprouts roots. Even better, there are so many varieties, such as pineapple mint, strawberry mint and chocolate peppermint, not to mention the basic peppermint and spearmint.

Ginger leaves can be used like mint, and it also makes a great house plant for a sunny, warm spot. It can be grown from an organic root, bought from a supermarket or food market: plant in a shallow tray until it sprouts, then pot on. See page 80 for advice on how to propagate ginger.

PLANTING

All these collections will be fine planted in multipurpose compost. Plant either singly in a collection of pots or all together in one window box or large trough planter. Prepare a small wigwam of canes for cucamelon to climb up and secure the plant to one of them; otherwise, let it trail over the side. Wayward stems can be snipped off.

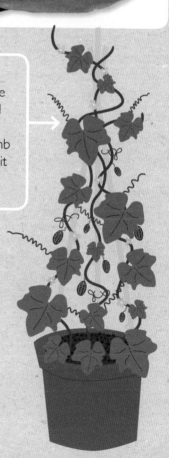

MAINTENANCE

Water as required, and feed throughout spring and summer. Regular picking will keep most herbs to size. When mint becomes pot-bound (i.e. the roots have filled the pot, leaving no room for them to expand), divide the plant into two or three new plants and pot up individually.

A HYDROPONIC SYSTEM OF SALADS

Hydroponic systems are a way of growing plants without using soil or compost. They are becoming increasingly common in the agricultural industry and are used in the growing number of urban farms, but can also be incredibly effective for growing at home.

WHAT DOES A HYDROPONIC SYSTEM LOOK LIKE?

In a hydroponic system, all the nutrients that soil would provide are given to the plant through water. It is a system commonly used in commercial glasshouses for growing salad vegetables, but is also useful in growing situations where compost or soil would be too heavy or bulky, such as roof gardens and living walls.

Sometimes the roots simply dangle in an ever-moving aerated stream of water and diluted fertiliser, and sometimes an inert growing medium, such as rock wool, is used to anchor the plants.

HYDROPONICS AT THEIR SIMPLEST

Many people will have been growing hydroponically without even realising it – the old childhood activity of growing cress 'hair' from an eggshell 'head' stuffed with damp cotton wool is essentially a form of hydroponic growing.

ADVANTAGES AND DISADVANTAGES FOR SHORT-TERM CROPS

Advantages

Hydroponics have many advantages. There is no messy compost and, especially when used in commercial environments, the nutrient balance for the plants can be adjusted to the perfect level, depending on the maturity of the crop and even the daily weather.

Once the system is in place, it also cuts down on costs. Lush growth can be quickly achieved due to the watering and feeding system. The use of artificial light means that crops can even be grown underground, which has the potential to revolutionise urban food supplies.

Disadvantages

Disadvantages include the environmental cost of the growing media, many of which are not biodegradable, and the initial capital outlay. The average home isn't going to be able to convert a room into a greenhouse using LED lights, heating fans, water circulation and feeding pipes just to grow a bit of salad for dinner! However, there are a number of small-scale set-ups that include lighting options for gloomier kitchens. These off-the-shelf products are ideal for a windowsill or desk space, and come with full instructions.

CREATING A DIY HYDRONIC SYSTEM

CREATING A DIY HYDROPONIC SYSTEM

Have a go at creating a home system using a bit of DIY.

The plants will need a container (such as a length of guttering that is higher at one end than the other).

They will also need a substrate (rock wool, perlite or similar) for their roots.

Water and diluted fertiliser can be poured into the guttering and allowed to flow down and out. A more complex system could collect the run-off in a tank and pump it back to the top.

You can find books on the specifics of hydroponic growing to help you, or seek out further guidance online (see the further resources on page 140).

WHAT TO PLANT

For growing some salad leaves, such as lettuce, rocket, mizuna and mibuna, hydroponic systems are a fun experiment. If there is sufficient space, they can also be used to grow tomatoes, cucumbers, chillies, peppers, annual herbs and wheatgrass.

Larger-scale
DIY hydroponic
systems can utilise
drip irrigation systems
and pumps.

A CLEANER, GREENER DESK SPACE

For those who work in grey, lifeless offices filled with the hum of assorted technology and overhead strip lighting, it will come as no surprise to learn that these environments are bad for human health. However, by simply introducing a few common house plants, it is possible to improve the air quality and create a more refreshing and relaxing work environment.

EVERYDAY POLLUTANTS

As long ago as 1989, NASA conducted a study on house plants to ascertain which species most effectively filtered and purified indoor air. The average urban office is likely to have high levels of pollutants in the air: either the windows cannot be opened, trapping all the emissions from the various machines within the office, or, if the windows can be opened, indoor pollutants are exchanged for external ones, such as vehicle exhaust fumes.

The worst offenders when it comes to chemicals in the air are trichloroethylene, xylene, formaldehyde, ammonia and benzene, which can variously cause symptoms from a relatively innocuous irritation to the eyes, nose and throat, to the more severe nausea, dizziness and fainting with prolonged and heavy exposure. These may sound like serious industrial chemicals, but they are found in everyday items, including some cleaning agents, printing inks, paint, exhaust fumes and even paper towels and tissues.

MADAGASCAR
DRAGON TREE

WHAT TO PLANT

A few well-placed plants on a desk and around the office can go a long way towards creating better air quality, as well as giving everyone some greenery on which to rest their eyes. The best plants to choose are:

Chinese evergreen (*Aglaonema modestum*)
Tail flower (*Anthurium andraeanum*)
Bamboo palm (*Chamaedorea seifrizii*)
Spider plant (*Chlorophytum comosum*)

SPIDER PLANT

Pot mum (*Chrysanthemum grandiflorum*)
Madagascar dragon tree (*Dracaena marginata*)
Benjamin tree (*Ficus benjamina*)
Barberton daisy (*Gerbera jamesonii*)
Common ivy (*Hedera helix*)
Lily turf (*Liriope*)
Boston fern (*Nephrolepis exaltata*)
Miniature date palm (*Phoenix roebelenii*)
Bamboo palm (*Rhapis excelsa*)
Mother-in-law's tongue (*Sansevieria trifasciata*)
Peace lily (*Spathiphyllum*)

All of these plants are sold commonly in garden centres, and all will filter at least one, if not several, of the pollutants from the air listed earlier. For desks with only space for one plant, choose *Sansevieria* or *Spathiphyllum*, as they are the ones that will filter all five of the worst toxins.

BAMBOO PALM

SPRING IN A TEACUP

Nothing says 'spring is on its way' more than the emergence of the first flowers of the season. Pretty, dainty flowers are ideal for a temporary spring display in vintage teacups. Plant up several to dot around a table or put on a cake stand for afternoon tea, or simply add them among other cups and jars on kitchen shelves.

OBTAINING PLANTS

Plants can be dug up from the garden or bought. Retailers commonly sell pots of flowering bulbs and perennials in spring, as individual species and also in larger mixed planters, which may be better value. Buy the smallest possible perennial plants – preferably as plug plants (sold for bedding plants).

The cups can be left as they are, but for a woodland feel, and a more attractive finish, cover the surface of the compost around the base of the plants with sphagnum moss, which is widely available in bags from garden centres. Arrange a layer of moss into each cup and use a spray bottle to mist it with water.

WHAT TO PLANT
- Common snowdrops (*Galanthus nivalis*)
- Daffodils (*Narcissus*)
- Grape hyacinth (*Muscari*)
- Early bulbous iris (*Iris reticulata*)

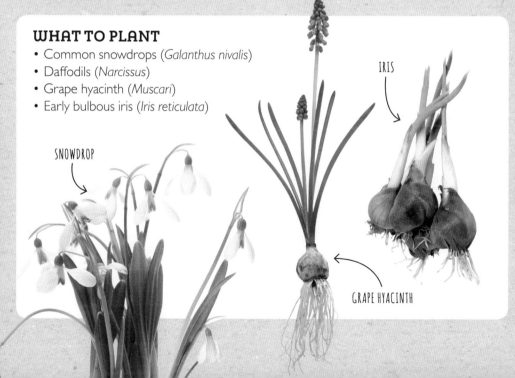

IRIS

SNOWDROP

GRAPE HYACINTH

METHOD

Remove the plants from their pots and crumble off as much of the compost from the roots as possible.

Arrange the plants into the teacups, either mixing the bulbs and perennials together or keeping to a single species within each cup. There should be room for a little layer of multipurpose compost in the base.

Fit as many plants as possible into each one, to get the fullest, best effect, and fill in around the edges with more compost to assure they fit firmly.

Water the cups so the compost is moist but not sodden – remember there is no drainage.

MAINTENANCE

The cups are best watered using a misting bottle, as this will keep the moss green, and a little water can percolate down to the roots of the plants and bulbs. They will need daily attention. Keep them in a bright spot (though they can be moved temporarily for display). The cooler the room, the longer the flowers will last. Once they have finished flowering, or the display is no longer required, both the bulbs and the perennials can be planted out into the garden.

CREATING HOUSE PLANTS FROM HOUSE PLANTS

The act of growing more plants is called propagation. Some house plants will do most of the work of propagating themselves. Others will readily grow into new plants from cuttings, or from a piece of root. Alternatively, they can be grown from external sources, such as a new pack of seeds.

Here are some of the simplest ways to create more house plants, which will produce a clone of the original plant. This is a great way to bulk up stock, replace older plants or make a lovely, personal gift.

SUCCULENT PUPS

Many succulents, such as *Aloe*, *Agave* and *Echeveria*, produce miniature versions of themselves, which grow from the side of the main plant. These baby plants are called 'offsets', or 'pups', and can be severed from the main plant and put into their own pot to grow and mature.

To propagate, simply cut away the pup, trying to keep as much root attached to it as possible, and plant into a small pot of compost and grit (see pages 112–115 for care of succulents).

SPIDER PLANTLETS

The long, dangling stems of mini plantlets are characteristic of the spider plant. In the wild, these would be looking to root themselves into something and grow into mature plants. To replicate this process at home, put a small pot of multipurpose compost under the first plantlet that is attached to a strong-looking stem (known as a 'runner') and cut off the rest of the stem beyond that plantlet.

If the plantlet will sit easily in the compost it can just be left. Otherwise, pin down the stem with a hair pin, or half a paperclip, which will keep the base of the plantlet just under the surface.

Keep the compost in the pot moist, and the plantlet should root into it relatively quickly. Once the plantlet is properly rooted into its own pot, cut off the stem/runner from both the mother plant and the plantlet. Pot on into a larger pot as it grows.

GINGER ROOTS

It is easy to grow ginger from 'roots' – technically rhizomes – bought from a supermarket. Use the plumpest, freshest-looking roots. Organic ones are preferable because commercial growth inhibitors are sometimes used on non-organic roots which can stop them sprouting once planted. You may find there are already some swollen buds visible.

Plant in a shallow pot in multipurpose compost, so that the root is about half submerged in the compost. Keep the compost moist and the pot in a very warm place (ideally 25–28°C). Shoots should sprout from the root. Once it is established in the shallow pot it can be potted up to a larger one. In the autumn, cut back the old stems as they die. Ginger is rated H1a for hardiness (see page 104).

PELARGONIUM CUTTINGS

A cutting is simply a small piece of healthy shoot that is cut off from the main plant and inserted into a pot of compost. It then produces roots and grows into a new plant. Several new plants can be created from a single original plant.

Scented pelargoniums are one of the easiest plants from which to take cuttings. The type of cutting used for pelargoniums is called a soft-wood cutting, as they are taken from the soft, flexible stems of the new growth.

Take pelargonium cuttings from healthy, well-watered plants in spring or summer. To increase your chances of success, cut a few shoots, but be sure to cut only leafy material – there should be no flowers or flower buds. Each cutting should be about 10cm long.

The base of each cutting should be just below a leaf joint ('node'). Remove the leaves with a sharp knife to leave a clear piece of stem at the base and a few leaves at the top. The soft tip of the shoot can also be pinched out.

Prepare a small pot with compost, large enough for a few cuttings to be planted. Clear a hole in the compost using a pencil, to avoid damaging the end of the cutting. Several cuttings can be spaced evenly around the edge of the pot. Once the cuttings have produced roots and are growing into their own plants, they can be potted up.

Water the pot and label it. Keep it in a warm and humid environment, with good but not direct sunlight. Use a covered heated propagator or fix a plastic bag over the top of the pot (with a support so that the bag is not touching the cuttings themselves), ensuring the cuttings are ventilated for a short while a couple of times a day. Alternatively, mist regularly.

A HELPING HORMONE

Before potting, you could dip the base of the cutting in hormonal rooting powder (available at garden centres), which will help the cuttings root.

CHAPTER 4

STAYING ALIVE

One of the joys of owning plants is looking after them. Having them just to look at and brighten up the room is brilliant, but the actual process of tending to and nurturing house plants can also bring much satisfaction and delight.

That said, looking after plants indoors can sometimes be as challenging as gardening outside – more, in fact – because although the environment is controlled, it is also enclosed and limited. However, the following pages should help avert any major crises.

Key to all gardening is keeping the plants happy and healthy. How to water and feed your house plants properly is also explained in this chapter. You will also find advice on what to do when you go away on holiday.

HOW TO KEEP PLANTS HEALTHY

Having a basic understanding of photosynthesis will lead to an appreciation of what plants need to grow and thrive.

PHOTOSYNTHESIS

In case school biology classes seem an awfully long time ago, these are the essential facts. Plants make their own food through a process called photosynthesis. To do this, they need light, water and carbon dioxide.

LIGHT

WATER

CARBON DIOXIDE

Limiting any one of these factors can lead to the plant struggling or even dying.

Plants photosynthesise using a chemical called chlorophyll — which is what makes plants look green — to absorb sunlight and turn the carbon dioxide and water into glucose (sugar) and oxygen. Some of the glucose is stored as starch, while the rest gets used up as energy for the plant to grow. A plant requires a range of nutrients to create chlorophyll for photosynthesis and other processes within the plant for healthy growth. Outside, there is plenty of sunlight, carbon dioxide and (with adequate rainfall) water, and the soil is able to provide the necessary nutrients. Indoors, gardeners need to provide water and nutrients, and to position the plant for adequate light.

APPLYING THE SCIENCE

Rule one when caring for any house plant is to put it in the environment in which it has evolved and to which it has adapted. In other words, a cactus that has evolved in the arid, sunny climate of a desert will not do well if it is kept in a shady, humid bathroom. Likewise, a Swiss cheese plant adapted to the lower levels of the tropical rainforest will not do well on a bright, cold and draughty windowsill.

THANK YOU!

Rule two is to try and make sure that the plant is never stressed by lack of water, light or nutrients, as this will weaken the plant and make it more susceptible to disease and pest infestation. Checking plants daily will take moments, but is far better for the plant than having to take remedial measures every now and then.

WATERING

House plants are often where most people start gardening, and their first taste of maintaining a plant is keeping them well watered. It is also where mistakes are commonly made. New gardeners can subsequently become downhearted and give up on trying to grow plants. However, watering really is not complicated!

WHEN TO WATER

First, check whether the plant needs watering. It sounds obvious, but this is where most of the mistakes get made. A plant and its compost can be deceiving in their looks; wilting leaves are not always a symptom of drought (leaves will also wilt when a plant is overwatered), and a moist compost surface can hide dryness beneath. It is therefore always, *always* worth checking properly if the plant actually needs water. No fancy equipment is needed – check by sticking your finger into the compost in the pot.

Too dry

If it feels dry and sandy, it needs water. Other signs that a plant needs watering include wilting leaves and stems, the flowers or buds dropping, and the drying compost shrinking away from the side of the pot.

Too wet

If it feels wet and squishy, it won't need water today (there are some specific exceptions to this, detailed in the Plant Files, pages 102–137). Check that there is no water pooling in the saucer underneath – if there is, pour it away and allow any further water to drain out of the pot.

Just right

If it feels moist, and a few particles stick to your finger, it will not need watering today, but check again tomorrow.

WATERING PROPERLY

To avoid potentially messy run-off or leaks when watering, temporarily move the plant to a basin or bath. When watering, the compost should be soaked thoroughly each time. Always water the compost, not the foliage, to ensure the water gets to where it is needed, and there is no excess humidity around the plant. Sprinkling a little water over the surface is insufficient and causes the roots grow up to the top of the pot, where they dry out faster. Watering too frequently or not allowing the excess water to drain away (i.e. letting water collect in a saucer under the pot, or the compost in a pot to become sodden) can kill a plant because the roots, which need access to oxygen, drown and rot in the waterlogged soil.

MISTING

Some house plants (see the Plant Files, pages 102–137) require some humidity around their leaves, which otherwise can turn dry, dull and crispy. Mist over and around the plant using a spray bottle, little and often, to maintain a good level of humidity and to avoid run-off onto surfaces.

FEEDING

A plant given sufficient light, water and carbon dioxide will survive, but for it to thrive it also needs nutrients – much like humans need a range of vitamins and minerals – which ensure the various and complex physiological processes work effectively. For house plants, the gardener must provide these nutrients, but fortunately this is a relatively simple task.

THE BIG THREE

The big three nutrients a plant needs are nitrogen, phosphorus and potassium, represented on a bottle of fertiliser by the letters N, P and K, respectively (the Latin, scientific name for potassium is *kalium*).

Nitrogen is needed for the production of cells and for the growth of leaves and shoots (yellowing leaves are a classic sign of nitrogen deficiency).

Phosphorus is needed for healthy root growth.

Potassium ensures good flower and fruit production.

On top of these, there are a range of necessary micronutrients, such as magnesium, boron and iron, which are needed in very small quantities but play important roles in cell production and photosynthesis.

WHEN TO FERTILISE

Plants bought from a garden centre or nursery will have been potted into compost that has all the necessary fertiliser mixed in to it, but the plant will exhaust this supply after around six months. After that, it will be necessary to apply fertiliser to maintain adequate nutrient levels. The myriad options available can be confusing, but the deciding factor is how long the fertiliser takes to release its nutrients.

The fastest-acting are the liquid fertilisers, because the nutrients can most easily be taken up by the plant. These can be be applied as a spray over the foliage or, more commonly and easily, as a concentrate that is then diluted and watered on. Liquid fertilisers need to applied regularly throughout the growing season, according to the instructions on the packet.

Slower or (more accurately) controlled-release fertilisers come as granules or small composite plugs of beads that are mixed with the soil surface or pushed into the pot, respectively. They are designed to break down over a period of weeks or months (again, check the packet for dosing instructions and longevity), releasing the nutrients inside as they go. However, the plugs do not always break down effectively, especially in soils that are kept on the dry side (such as with arid plants).

In general, fertilising is only necessary in the growing season, but specifics are listed with each plant in the Plant Files chapter (pages 102–137).

CLEANING

Outside, rain doesn't just provide water to the plants; it also washes off dust, fallen petals, pollen, dead insects and other detritus that can collect on the leaves of a plant. In doing so, it keeps the sunlight-absorption rates of the leaves as high as possible.

Inside, of course, there is no rain to provide that service for house plants, and also potentially a lot more dust that can accumulate on their leaves. A little cleaning now and then keeps the plants bright and healthy, and also removes any pests that might have taken up residence.

HOW TO CLEAN

Cleaning methods depend on the plant type and size. A delicate maidenhair fern cannot be cleaned in the same way as a thick and waxy-leaved fig. There is no right way to go about it, just deploy common sense and the available materials. For most, a quick shower is sufficient – though for the most delicate-leaved, use a misting spray bottle rather than a power shower. Direct the shower up from underneath, as well, to clean the undersides of the leaves.

If a plant hasn't been cleaned in a while, has got a little greasy as well as dusty (common for kitchen plants) and/or has large waxy leaves on which water spots would be apparent, combine the shower with a gentle rub using a soft cloth or piece of kitchen paper along the top and bottom of the leaf. Hold and support the leaf on the other side as you do this to avoid breaking or damaging it. Water-based baby wipes, without added fragrances or chemicals, are also great for wiping leaves. For the most delicate and intricate plants, such as succulents, use a soft paintbrush to dust the leaves, or a damp cotton bud to clean them.

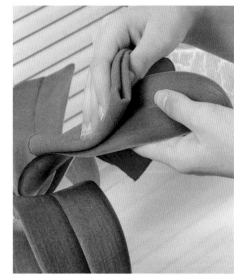

Leave plants to drip-dry away from direct sunlight, as they may scorch, before returning them to their usual spot. If limescale spots could be a problem, dry each leaf carefully with a soft (microfibre) cloth.

'LEAF SHINE'

It is possible to purchase a polishing spray – 'leaf shine' – that can be used to clean and polish leaves in one go, giving them a shiny and spot-free appearance, but these are best avoided because they can block the pores, leaving the leaves unable to absorb carbon dioxide.

GOING ON HOLIDAY

Ideally, a friend or neighbour is able to step in to water and feed your plants as required. It is perhaps a good idea to first offer them a run-through, or leave instructions by each pot. However, if nobody is available to help, there are various measures that can be taken to care for the plants left behind when you go away.

PRE-DEPARTURE CHECKS

Always check plants thoroughly for pest and diseases in the week leading up to the holiday, and deal with them then, otherwise they will enjoy the holiday as well. Water and feed the plants thoroughly before you leave.

MOVE THEIR POTS

Moving plants away from windows means that they will be out of direct sunlight (which dries them out) in the summer, and safe from cold draughts in the winter. In the summer, move the plants to the coolest room, and in winter to the warmest (assuming the heating will be turned off). Fridges and freezers give off heat, and in the absence of central heating, it can be a good idea if you go away in winter to put plants on top of these appliances.

CAPILLARY MATTING

WATERING SYSTEMS

While dormant in winter, many house plants will tolerate a few days without water, providing they are given a thorough watering before you depart for a holiday. However, in the summer, many plants will need constant access to water, without becoming waterlogged.

Plants take up water through their roots, and in doing so draw it through the soil. Capillary matting is a means of extending the reach of the roots into a well of water collected in, for example, a bath, sink, large bowl or deep roasting tin. As the soil in the pot becomes dry, the water is drawn up from the well through the matting and into the pot.

One option is to place the pot directly onto the matting and have it dangle over the side into the well. For instance, place a washing-up bowl full of water in the sink with the plants on the matting on the draining board above. This works best with plastic pots; for terracotta pots, push the matting up into the drainage hole to ensure a better connection.

Alternatively, push a strip of the matting into the compost in the top of the pot. This will act as a wick, drawing up moisture from an individual well, and would be a good option for larger or more delicate plants that cannot be moved easily.

RAISING HUMIDITY

Grouping plants together will help reduce water loss from the plants. All plants give off water through transpiration – evaporation of water through the stomata (pores) in the leaves. The drier the air, the faster the water loss. Grouping plants together means the surrounding air becomes more humid than if they were to be individually placed; hence the evaporation gradient is flatter and the water loss slowed. For short absences, tie a clear plastic bag around the whole plant and pot, using canes inserted into the pot to keep the bag from touching the leaves.

KEEPING PLANTS TIDY

When a house plant becomes a little too happy in its situation, some action may be required to keep it from taking over the house. To an extent, not being in its ideal outdoor environment (for example, a dry, cool living room rather than a tropical jungle) will keep a house plant's size under control. Restricting the roots in a pot and not over-feeding will also help. However, to further control a plant's size, it can be pruned, either above or below ground.

ROOT PRUNING

Root pruning is simple and best done in spring when the plant is growing well. Remove the plant from the pot. Use a sharp kitchen knife to shave off a couple of centimetres of roots and compost all the way round the root ball, then put it back into the pot with some fresh compost to fill the gaps.

PROMOTING FLOWERS AND A BETTER SHAPE

Pruning is also done to make plants more attractive – to promote a better shape, or more flowering. Plants that would naturally grow leggy, single stems, such as geraniums or chrysanthemums, can be pinched out as they grow. This will encourage a bushier shape that bears more flowers. Regularly snip or pinch out the tips of new growth. This method also works well for herbs.

CLIMBING AND LARGER PLANTS

Climbers and trailing plants can have their shoots cut back when they reach the extent of their supports, or start getting in the way. Trimming little and often is better than an infrequent drastic cut back. Likewise, pruning the woody stems of larger plants is better done by cutting back no more than a third at a time.

The guiding principles should be:
• Always cut back to just above a bud.
• Refer to the individual plant's requirements in the Plant Files of this book (pages 102–137) or on the RHS website.
• Learn how to best care for plants through observation of their growing habits in their unique situation.
• Think twice and cut once.

GENERAL HOUSEKEEPING

All house plants will shed old leaves at some point. Remove these and any other detritus, and promptly cut back dead stems to avoid rot setting in, which can spread to the plant, and to retain a healthy, green appearance.

PESTS

Pests can infect a house plant even in the most sterile and urban environments, but it would defeat the object to have plants permanently covered and protected. A few of the usual suspects are listed below, but see also the further resources (page 140) for where to find more information on identifying and dealing with pests.

PREVENTION IS BETTER THAN CURE

Keeping plants healthy — well-watered, fertilised and in the correct position — will help them fight off attacks from bugs and other pests. Catching an infestation early increases the chances of getting rid of it, so check plants regularly. It's also crucial to check whether there are pests on any other plants that are in the house, or those being brought into the house.

Use chemical pesticides only as a last resort after trying the other control methods, and always select a treatment that is recommended for the problem. Read the labels of any chemicals, and make sure that all the manufacturer's instructions are followed, including maximum dose, spray and harvest intervals.

MEALY BUG AND SCALE INSECTS

Very hard to get rid of once they take hold, mealy bugs live in the nooks and crannies of plants and are covered in a waxy white fluff. Scale insects can be found on the undersides of leaves and on stems, under a dome of brown wax, making them impervious to washing and sprays.

Signs of damage: Both suck the sap and so make plants appear stunted and generally unhealthy. The plant can also be coated with clear, sticky excrement (known as 'honeydew').

Controlling the problem: Pick off those that can be seen. Blasting robust plants with a shower will dislodge a few more, but make sure those removed are washed away completely. Chemical and biological treatments are also available. If the plant is particularly valuable, it may be necessary to tolerate and control a low-level infestation to avoid losing it.

APHIDS AND WHITEFLY

Greenfly and blackfly take the sap from leaves and stems. Whitefly is not an aphid, but the damage and control caused are much the same.

Signs of damage: curling, wilting or distorted leaves and young stems; sticky leaves that can later develop a black mould on the surface; clusters of bugs around the freshest growth; whitefly will rise in a cloud from the plant if disturbed.

APHIDS

Controlling the problem: physically wash or pick them off, removing them completely, not just depositing them onto the soil, or they'll climb back up; treat with proprietary sprays and insecticidal soaps.

DISEASES

House plant diseases tend to be fungal rather than bacterial or viral, and the most likely are listed here. If the symptoms don't match, check the further resources (page 140) for where to find more information.

A HEALTHY ENVIRONMENT

As with preventing pests, infection is much less likely on healthy plants, so look after the house plants well. Good housekeeping is also important to avoid cultivating an atmosphere in which disease could take hold, and to avoid spreading any existing disease. Keep plants tidy, removing dead leaves and other detritus from around the base of the plant. Make sure tools and equipment – including the pots themselves – are clean by washing with soap or other detergent and hot water. If the plant's compost develops mould on its surface, repot it, washing off the roots entirely before replanting in fresh compost.

Fungicidal sprays are available to treat some diseases, but are best reserved for only when they are absolutely necessary. Select a treatment that is recommended for the disease you have identified and always read the label before choosing a product. Make sure that all the manufacturer's instructions are followed, including maximum dose, spray and harvest intervals.

BOTRYTIS

Also known as grey mould and, to wine-makers, noble rot. Spores are ever-present in the air, everywhere, and readily infect dead or weak tissue, before spreading to the rest of the plant.

Signs of damage: Fluffy grey mould developing quickly on leaves and stems, or spots on petals.

Control: Prevent infection with good air circulation and by promptly removing dead or damaged tissue with neat cuts to minimise open wounds. Remove and dispose of infected tissue, trying to contain it in the process, to avoid spreading more clouds of spores.

MILDEW

Both powdery and downy mildews are fungal diseases that cause white mould on leaf surfaces.

Signs of damage: Patches of white mould – powdery on the upperside, downy on the underside with corresponding yellow patches above. Leaves yellow and die; growth is inhibited.

Control: Powdery mildew often infects plants with dry roots and humid leaves, so ensure good air circulation and correct watering. Downy mildew is also characteristic of damp environments and often infects young plants. Remove affected parts as soon as they are seen and improve the atmosphere around the plant.

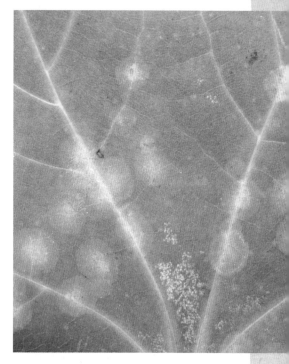

VIRUSES

These tend to be brought in via the plant or occasionally through infected pests or tools.

Signs of damage: The whole plant will become stunted and/or distorted, with yellow spots or streaks on the leaves.

Control: It's impossible to treat a virus, so the plant must be disposed of and all tools and equipment thoroughly cleaned afterwards to avoid the infection spreading to other plants.

OTHER POTENTIAL PROBLEMS

Aside from pests and diseases, house plants may suffer or become damaged, but these problems are the most easily rectified.

WATERING

Lack of, or a surfeit of, water can cause a plant to wilt and is easily the most common problem house plants suffer from. Refer to pages 86–87 for how best to go about watering.

NUTRIENT DEFICIENCY

Symptoms of a nutrient deficiency will depend on what particular nutrients are deficient. However, most commonly, nitrogen and magnesium deficiencies will show as a yellowing of the leaves, starting with the oldest leaves first (if it's magnesium, the veins will remain green).

A potassium deficiency will be evident from poor flowering and fruiting, and phosphorus deficiency by a blueish tinge and poor root development. Treat any nutrient deficiency with the appropriate application of fertiliser, always within the dosage and frequency advised on the packet. See pages 88–89 for more information on how to feed plants.

LEAF SCORCH

If the edges of the leaves turn brown and crispy, they have died suddenly due to extremes of either heat or cold. This is most common in plants on windowsills. The damaged leaves cannot be saved, but allow them to fall off naturally, as the plant may still be withdrawing nutrients from them. Dispose of the leaves once fallen and shelter the plant from whatever has caused the damage – remove from direct sunlight, radiator heat or cold draughts, for example. Brown tips can be snipped off to retain the rest of the leaf.

PHYSICAL DAMAGE

Broken branches or stems, or frayed or eaten leaves, are generally caused by knocks from passers-by, such as children or pets. Cut off broken sections to leave a clean cut in healthy tissue, and consider moving the plant to a more protected position.

POT-BOUND

The plant will grow slowly, if at all, when pot-bound, even when given proper watering and feeding, and roots may protrude from the drainage hole. Lifting the plant out of the pot will reveal the congested, circling roots. Repot into a larger container, or prune the roots if repotting is not an option.

CHAPTER 5

PLANT FILES

The following pages list some of the most interesting, most reliable and commonly available house plants and their requirements. They are divided into groups according to how much light and humidity they need. While these factors will to some extent influence the temperature of the room, taking into account the various microclimates in the home, the key will give further guidance on how warm the spot should be.

This is just a taster of the variety of wonderful house plants available – once bitten by the bug, you may wish to seek out more unusual plants!

KEY TO THE PLANT FILES

Each plant is listed by its common name first, followed by its botanical Latin name. The key gives information on its growth habit (a climber, for example), likely height and spread – although these measurements are given as an approximate guide to the plant's ultimate (mature) size, and most house plants will take many years to reach this.

The temperature ratings indicated in the key are the same as the RHS hardiness ratings, which can be found below and on the RHS website. The key also indicates the plant's most attractive feature (such as flower, foliage or an edible crop).

KEY

H1a = a warm room (min.15°C).
H1b = a temperate room. Plants can be put outside for summer when night-time temperatures are sufficiently high (10 to 15°C).
H1c = a cool room. Plants can be put outside in the summer (5 to 10°C).
H2 = frost-free greenhouse or cold room (1 to 5°C).
H3 = unheated greenhouse (-5 to 1°C).
H4 = outside in an average UK winter (-10 to -5°C).
H5 = outside in a cold UK winter (-15 to -10°C).
H6 = outside in a cold UK winter (-20 to -15°C). Pots may still need protection.

A = annual plant
B = biennial plant
Bu = bush
C = crop
Car = carnivorous
Cl = climber
F = flowers
Fe = fern
H = ultimate height
L = foliage
Orc = orchid
Pa = palm
P = perennial plant

S = ultimate spread
Suc = succulent
Tr = tree
Trai = trailing

CHRISTMAS CACTUS

SUNNY SPOTS

These plants will do well in direct sunlight, such as on a south-facing windowsill, in a conservatory or other bright room. No indoor space can compete with the light levels of outside – even a glasshouse has lower light levels because of the filtering effect of the glass – but give these plants the sunniest spot in the house, and they will prosper. The room should have a relatively dry and/or airy atmosphere, though some of these plants like it sunny and humid, so they will need misting.

Bougainvillea
Bougainvillea
H1b, P, F, Cl
H 4–8m **S** 1–1.5m
This is a vigorous plant that will need plenty of space, but can be trained easily on supports or wires. Bright flowers (actually bracts) appear in summer, which come in a range of colours, depending on species and variety – all can be treated the same. Protect from midday summer sun and mist in hot situations/rooms. Water regularly in summer but sparingly in winter. Feed in summer. Prune back side-shoots in autumn.

Crimson bottlebrush
Callistemon citrinus 'Splendens'
H3, P, F, L, Bu
H 4–8m **S** 2.5–4m
A South African plant that will survive outside in a sheltered position, *Callistemon* is slow-growing and also makes a good low-maintenance house plant. Bright red bottle-brush flowers are borne in spring and summer, and the foliage is fragrant. Water regularly in summer but sparingly in winter. Feed in summer. Only needs pruning to remove damaged, dead or wayward shoots.

Chilli pepper
Capsicum annuum
H1c, A, C, Bu
H 1m **S** 0.5m
Attractive, temporary house plants for sunny windowsills, and come with the added bonus of a harvest of chillies. There are many varieties available, so choose according to preferred size, colour and heat level ('Nu-Mex Twilight', for example, is an attractive, compact plant). Sow seeds in a heated propagator in late winter, and pot on, giving the mature plant a 2-litre pot. Pinch out growing tips to create bushier growth and mist when flowering to aid pollination. Chillies are mature when firm to a squeeze and ripe when they reach their final colour.

CALLISTEMON

Chillies make colourful and productive house plants.

Citrus
Citrus
H1b, P, F, L, C, Tr
H 1–1.5m **S** 1m

Including lemons, limes, oranges, grapefruits and more, all citrus trees can be grown in a large pot indoors, though they will appreciate being outside in the summer, if possible. *Citrus × limon* 'Meyer' (Meyer's lemon) and *Fortunella margarita* (Nagami kumquat) are good compact trees. Water freely in summer, sparingly in winter. Feed in summer. Misting can help pollination. Prune only to pinch out shoots (to encourage bushy growth) and to remove dead and side-shoots borne on and at the base of the stem.

Cigar plant
Cuphea ignea
H2, P, F, Bu
H 0.4m **S** 0.5–1m

A spreading evergreen sub-shrub with pointed leaves. The flowers are tubular, and red with a black-and-white tip, hence the common name. Cigar plant is often sold as a tender bedding plant, or can be grown from seed. Water as required and feed in summer. Only prune to remove dead or damaged shoots, and to pinch out growing tips on young plants.

PELARGONIUM

Tropical hibiscus
Hibiscus rosa-sinensis
H1b, P, F, Bu
H 2m **S** 1m

Evergreen hibiscus that makes a shrubby house plant (unlikely to reach its full height, unless in very good conditions) with showy flowers. Individual flowers do not last long, but are regularly produced through the summer. Needs plenty of light, but protect from midday summer sun. Mist regularly to maintain humidity. Water regularly in summer, sparingly in winter. Feed in summer. Prune in late winter or early spring, shortening all shoots back to a good framework and removing those that are overcrowded.

Pelargonium
Pelargonium
H1c, P, F, L, C, Bu
H 1m **S** 1m

Sometimes mistakenly referred to as 'geraniums', these fall into two groups, both suitable as house plants. One is grown primarily for flowers (commonly red or white, though their bi-colour leaves are also attractive), the other for their scented leaves (bright and crinkled leaves, scented with anything from rose, lemon and apples to cloves and cinnamon). On the latter, the leaves and summer flowers (pink or white tones) are smaller, but can be used in the kitchen. Water and feed regularly in summer, sparingly in winter. Cut back to a short, open framework each spring.

Dwarf pomegranate
Punica granatum var. *nana*
H3, P, F, L, Bu
H 1m **S** 1m

Although fully hardy, the dwarf pomegranate makes a slow-growing, rounded, compact shrub that is a lovely house plant. It is deciduous, bringing some seasonality not often seen in house plants. It flowers in summer, bearing fruit into the autumn. Water and feed regularly in summer, sparingly in winter. Prune only to remove dead or damaged shoots.

Hibiscus flowers are short-lived but abundant.

COLEUS

Coleus
Solenostemon
H1b, P, L, Bu
H 1m **S** 1m

Perennial plants, often treated as annuals, though can be over-wintered. Their serrated leaves come in a wide range of wonderful colours and patterns – it's possible to buy seed mixes that give a good spread of colours within one packet. Protect from direct sun on hot summer days, and mist frequently to maintain high humidity. Pinch out growing shoots of young plants to encourage bushy growth. Seed can be sown in spring, or over-wintered plants can be cut back to a short framework in spring.

Coriander
Coriandrum sativum
H5, A, L, C, Bu
H&S 0.1–0.5m

Widely used in many cuisines. Easily grown from seed. For fresh leaves, use bolt-resistant varieties such as 'Leisure'. Seeds are easily produced by any stressed plant; alternatively, use the variety 'Moroccan', which has been developed for good seed production. Water well and give seedlings plenty of space to avoid bolting. Sow successively from spring for a regular supply of leaves and a good crop of seeds by the autumn.

Basil
Ocimum basilicum
H1c, A, L, C, Bu
H&S 0.1–0.5m

A staple of continental cookery. Sow seeds from spring to early summer for a regular supply. Seeds give the best range of varieties, but supermarket-bought potted plants can also be divided and replanted to give a good crop. For pesto, grow 'Genovese', for Asian dishes 'Siam Queen' and for ornamental plants 'Purple Ruffles' and 'African Blue'. For a more intense flavour and bushier plant, try Greek basil (*O. minimum*). Lemon basil (*O. x citriodorum*) is also an alternative worth trying.

Flat-leaved parsley
Petroselinum crispum var. *neopolitanum*
H6, B, L, C, Bu
H&S 0.1–0.5m

A biennial but best treated as annual because the leaves become coarser with age. Easily grown from seed or from potted-on supermarket plants. Sow seed from spring through summer. Parsley will take a cooler and shadier spot than most other herbs.

Rosemary
Rosmarinus officinalis
H4, P, L, C, Bu
H&S 1.5–2.5m

Rosemary's aromatic leaves have a wide range of uses. Regular snipping of the shoots for the kitchen will keep the plant compact, though they are best replaced every five years or so to prevent the lower stems becoming woody and sprawling. 'Miss Jessop's Upright' is a slightly more upright and compact form. When potting on, include some grit in the compost to aid drainage. Never allow to sit in sodden compost.

Thyme
Thymus vulgaris
H5, P, L, C, Bu
H&S 0.1–0.5m

Thyme's aromatic leaves have a wide range of uses. As with rosemary, regular snipping of the shoots will keep the plant compact, but it is best to replace every five years or so to prevent the lower stems becoming woody and sprawling. When potting on, include some grit in the compost to aid drainage. Never allow to sit in sodden compost. An alternative thyme plant to try growing is lemon thyme.

Rosemary will thrive on a sunny windowsill.

SUCCULENTS

Succulents, which include cacti, characteristically can store water in fleshy leaves or stems to use during periods of drought, which can make them forgiving house plants. They are also by and large slow growing, and therefore ideal for small spaces. Most will flourish in full sun, taking the hottest of positions in the house. However, some (*Schlumbergia, Rhipsalis, Epiphyllum,* for example) are natural forest dwellers that grow as epiphytes on tree trunks and will prefer a partially shaded, more humid spot. There is a huge range of cacti available, so choose according to your preferred shapes and colours. Cacti can also produce flowers, but this can take up to twenty years, so if this is desired, buy mature plants or those that are known to have flowered already.

Use a multipurpose compost mixed in equal quantities with horticultural grit, or buy a proprietary cactus compost. Repot only into a slightly larger pot each time to avoid swamping the plants. Water regularly in spring and summer, as for any other plant, but be sure that the excess has fully drained away so that the compost does not become sodden, and allow it to dry out between watering times. Feed in summer, using either a proprietary cactus fertiliser or a general balanced liquid fertiliser. In winter, if the room is cool (consider moving them if not), most desert cacti and succulents will rest and need very little watering.

Agave
Agave
H1b, P, L, Suc
H&S 1m
With long triangular fleshy leaves in an approximate rosette and thorns along the edges, agaves are the genus from which tequila is made. Grey-green American aloe (*Agave americana*) is the most common, and has a variegated form, but glaucous Parry's agave (*Agave parryi*) is more compact and has stunning black edged-leaves.

Aloe
Aloe
H1c, P, L, Suc
H&S 0.5–1m
The most common form of *Aloe* is *Aloe vera* (also known as Barbados aloe), with its maple-leaf silhouette of narrow green leaves, but candelabra aloe (*Aloe arborescens*) can make a more attractive, upright and compact plant. All species bear spines, but these are not generally sharp except on Cape aloe (*Aloe ferox*). Flower spikes of red/orange flowers are possible, but not guaranteed.

AGAVE

A gravel mulch will help reflect light onto sun-loving succulents.

Many succulents
have similar
requirements and
can be mixed in
a planter.

Money tree
Crassula ovata
H1c, P, L, Suc
H&S 2m

This succulent forms a tree shape, with a brown trunk and branches bearing ovate dark-green fleshy leaves. It grows slowly and can bear pretty white flowers (it is said that if it flowers then the owner will come into some money).

Echeveria
Echeveria
H1c, P, L, Suc
H&S 0.2m

Although echeveria produce flowers more freely than other succulents (usually red/orange on a long stem) they are grown for their rosettes of foliage. Good examples include *E. elegans* (blue and white foliage), *E. secunda* var. *glauca* (blue and green) and *E.* 'Black Prince' (dark purple). They grow by producing new rosettes that multiply out sideways. These can be severed and grown on as new plants – preferable, in fact, as the rosettes look best in isolation in a small pot.

Pebble plant
Lithops
H1c, P, L, Suc
H&S 0.1m

Known as living stones, the leaves (the size of which differs between species) are virtually cylindrical and grey, with some mottling, and are supplemented by white daisy flowers in late summer or early autumn.

Christmas cactus
Schlumbergera
H1b, P, L&F, Suc
H&S 0.5m

A common house plant or gift at Christmas time (hence the name), when generally it is in flower (varieties of red, pink and white). Despite the name, it hails from the rainforest, and needs a partially shaded, humid position.

Kalanchoe
Kalanchoe
H1b, P, L, F, Suc
H&S 0.5m

Most commonly available is flaming Katy (*K. blossfeldiana*) and its hybrids, which make compact house plants. Their dark-green leaves are easily scorched in direct sun, so place in partial shade. Clusters of flowers (shades of red, orange or yellow) are borne in spring, but commonly sold in flower all year round.

MONEY TREE

BRIGHT SPOTS

These plants need a good level of light, but not direct sunlight. The ambient temperature is, therefore, lower than for the plants in the 'Sunny Spots' section, and although again they do not generally require high humidity, some may benefit from an occasional misting.

Pineapple
Ananas comosus
H1a, P, Bu/Suc, L, (C)
H&S 0.3m
It is possible to buy ornamental pineapples that sometimes bear small fruits, but it's cheaper and more fun to try rooting the top of a fresh pineapple bought from a local grocers or supermarket. Twist off the top and remove the lower leaves. Suspend the bare stem in water and wait for roots to appear before potting in a 50/50 compost and grit mix. Water as required and feed in the summer. Prune only to remove dead leaves.

Bird's nest fern
Asplenium nidus
H1b, P, L, Fe
H&S 1.5m
The bird's nest fern is a very tolerant plant, making it an ideal beginner's house plant. The large flat, glossy leaves are mid-green and have an attractive black midrib and crinkled edges. Pot using a mix of 75/25 multipurpose compost and grit, and water as required. Clean the leaves regularly to keep them clean and shiny. Prune only to cut out dead leaves to the base; brown edges can also be trimmed.

Dwarf mountain palm
Chamaedorea elegans
H1a, P, L, Pa
H 2.5m **S** 1.5m
A staple of home stores and garden centre house plant sales, the dwarf mountain palm makes an attractive house plant and is usually available to buy in various sizes. The long pinnate leaves are borne on slender stems, earning the plant its 'elegant' name well. Water regularly in summer, sparingly in winter. Feed monthly in summer. Prune only to remove dead leaves.

Dwarf fan palm
Chamaerops humilis
H4, P, L, Pa
H&S 1.5m
This palm is fully hardy, but also grows well indoors (it can be moved outside for the summer). It is squat rather than elegant, and has fan-shaped leaves on spiny stalks. Older specimens will have a fibrous trunk. Water regularly in summer, sparingly in winter. Feed monthly in summer. Prune only to remove dead leaves.

DWARF FAN PALM

New leaves unfurl from the base of the bird's nest fern.

Natal lily
Clivia miniata
H1c, P, L, F, Bu
H 0.4m, **S** 0.3m

Strappy, dark-green leaves are the perfect foil for the bright orange and red tones of the flower spikes on a *Clivia*. The flowers, borne in spring and summer, are lily-like, and the plant needs a colder spell to produce them, so a conservatory with more seasonal temperature variations is ideal. Water regularly in summer, sparingly in winter. Feed monthly in summer. Prune only to remove dead leaves and flower spikes.

Arabian coffee
Coffea arabica
H1b, P, L, Bu
H 0.6m, **S** 0.5m

It is unlikely that coffee grown as a house plant will actually produce any useable beans but, regardless, the plant is attractive with glossy, crinkled leaves and a good curio. 'Grow your own coffee plant' kits and packets of just the seed are available from online suppliers. Alternatively, buy a ready-grown plant. Pinch out the growing tip of young plants to encourage bushy growth. Water regularly in summer, sparingly in winter. Feed monthly in summer. Prune only to remove dead leaves.

Madagascar dragon tree
Dracaena marginata
H1b, P, L, Pa
H 3m **S** 2m

Madagascar dragon tree is widely available either in its basic form, which has green/red leaves, or as the 'Tricolor' variety, which has cream-edged leaves. Both bear clumps of arching, strappy leaves atop a slender trunk, with plants usually sold with two or three trunks per pot at different heights. Water regularly in summer, sparingly in winter. Feed monthly in summer. Prune only to remove dead leaves. If the room is very dry, an occasional misting will help.

Flat palm
Howea forsteriana
H1a, P, L, Pa
H 8–1m **S** 4–8m

One for a larger room, as it can reach sizeable proportions, but its young growth is relatively upright. The broad leaves are divided (i.e. pinnate) and borne on slender stems. Water regularly in summer, sparingly in winter. Feed monthly in summer. Prune only to remove dead leaves.

Four-leaved pink sorrel
Oxalis tetraphylla
H1c, P, L, F, Bu
H 0.2m, **S** indefinite

Some *Oxalis* species are serious garden weeds, but contained as a house plant they are rather pretty. Their clover-like leaves are sometimes supplemented by red/purple flowers in summer. Water regularly in summer, sparingly in winter. Feed monthly in summer. Prune only to remove dead leaves and flowers.

COFFEE

Clivia's bright
flowers are offset
by its glossy
dark leaves.

Mother-in-law's
tongue — sharp and
persistent!

Mother-in-law's tongue
Sansevieria trifasciata
H1b, P, L, Bu
H 1.5m **S** 0.5m

Mother-in-law's tongue grows as an upright clump of lanceolate, fleshy leaves that are predominantly green but have yellow margins and some yellow patterning. Pot in a 50/50 compost/grit mix (plants can be easily divided if getting too big for the space). Water regularly in summer, sparingly in winter. Feed monthly in summer. Prune only to remove dead leaves.

Peace lily
Spathiphyllum wallisii
H1b, P, L, Bu
H&S 0.5m

The peace lily forms clumps of dark-green ovate leaves and white flowers (spathes). All parts of the plant are extremely toxic. Water regularly in summer, sparingly in winter. Feed monthly in summer. Prune only to remove dead leaves and flowers. It will benefit from an occasional misting.

Bird of paradise
Strelitzia reginae
H1b, P, F, Bu
H 1.5m **S** 1m

Bird of paradise plants are aptly named and make a spectacular house plant. Bright orange and purple flowers emerge from tall spikes with beak-like buds, set off well by the slightly glaucous paddle-shaped foliage. Water regularly in summer, sparingly in winter. Feed monthly in spring and summer. Prune only to remove dead leaves and flower spikes. Mist occasionally.

Cape primrose
Streptocarpus
H1b, P, F, Bu
H 0.3m **S** 0.5m

This plant has a primrose-like flower borne on delicate stems above long, slightly furry, dark-green leaves. Varieties available can include pastel-pink, blue or purple flowers (visit a specialist nursery for the best choice). Best watered from a saucer to avoid rotting leaves, but do not allow to stand wet. Water regularly in summer, sparingly in winter. Feed monthly in summer. Prune only to remove dead leaves and trim flower spikes back to the base.

BIRD OF PARADISE

ORCHIDS

Different species will suit assorted room conditions. They are grown not for their foliage but for their long-lasting displays of beautiful, delicate and intricate flowers. Orchids like high humidity around their leaves, but do not like to sit in wet compost. The best compost option is a free-draining potting mix consisting largely of bark chips (buy a proprietary orchid compost). Keep the plant in a pot with drainage holes. Its roots will also protrude above the pot but don't be tempted to tidy them inside because if you do they will rot.

Water thoroughly about once a week, ensuring all excess has drained away, and mist to supplement humidity where required. Feed using a specialist orchid fertiliser once a month during spring and summer. Keep the leaves clean. Prune only to remove dead leaves, flower spikes and roots.

Moth orchid
Phalaenopsis
H1a, P, F, Orc
H 1m **S** 0.3m
Give this plant bright but not direct light. Avoid fluctuating temperatures, although flowering can be induced by moving to a cooler room for a month. Produces tall spikes of flowers from flat, almost rectangular rosettes of dark-green waxy leaves. Flowers can last for months, and colours vary between varieties. Prune the spike back to its second joint below the flowers once they've finished, and it may produce a secondary spike.

Cymbidium
Cymbidium
H1c, P, F, Orc
H&S 0.9m
Similar flowers to moth orchid but leaves are tall and strappy. Give this plant bright but not direct light. As flower spikes develop, keep the temperature below 15°C, otherwise the buds can drop off prematurely.

Vanda
Vanda
H1b, P, F, Orc
H 1m **S** 0.5m
Best grown in an open-weave or slatted basket, out of which their roots can hang, species of *Vanda* have a flat, fan-shaped rosette of leaves. The flower spike is produced from the top of this rosette. Allow bright but not direct light and relatively humid conditions – supplement by misting the roots daily, more often if very dry, but always allowing to dry them out between watering. Feed by misting with a diluted fertiliser or plunging in a diluted solution for 10 minutes once a week.

CYMBIDIUM

Phalaenopsis orchids are inexpensive and beautiful house plants.

SHADY AND HUMID SPOTS

These plants are ideal for a poorly lit bathroom or even a kitchen that regularly gets steamy. They still need some light and plants in particularly dark rooms may benefit from being rotated with another, better-lit, spot regularly to recover, but all these plants will thrive in a partially shaded and relatively humid atmosphere.

Delta maidenhair fern
Adiantum raddianum
H1c, P, L, Fe
H&S 0.5m
This is one of the most delicate ferns, with black stems bearing tiny leaflets that tremble in the slightest breeze. A slightly scented-leaved version, 'Fragrantissimum', is also available. Water regularly and feed with a diluted fertiliser in spring and summer. Prune only to remove dead fronds.

Spider plant
Chlorophytum comosum
H2, P, L, Bu
H&S 0.5m
A popular and easy house plant, the spider plant bears flowers on runners which, much like a strawberry plant, also have little plantlets along their length that can be potted up to make new plants. Arching, thin leaves are striped with white and can extend over and below a container. Water regularly from spring to autumn, sparingly in winter. Feed in the summer. Prune only to remove dead leaves or unwanted runners.

Croton
Codiaeum variegatum
H1b, P, L, Bu
H 1.5m **S** 1m
A great jungle-type plant, and a good one for children, the leathery leaves are veined with red, orange or yellow depending on the variety (the colour can also change as the leaves age), offset by the dark purple-green of the rest of the leaf. Water regularly. Feed in summer and prune to remove dead leaves. To stimulate bushier growth, leggy plants can be cut back so the stems are only 10cm high.

Ornamental fig
Ficus
H1c, P, L, Bu or Tr
H 2m **S** 1m
This is a wide-ranging genus of house plants, including the rubber plant (*F. elastica*), which has large glossy, oval leaves usually on a single stem, and the weeping fig (*F. benjamina*), with its pendulous branches of pointy, oval-shaped leaves. Creeping fig (*F. pumila*) and *F. sagittata* are both trailing varieties. All species of *Ficus* are relatively forgiving plants and, unless given optimum conditions, will be quite slow-growing. Water regularly in summer, sparingly in winter. Feed in the summer. Prune only to remove dead branches and to restrict size.

SPIDER PLANT

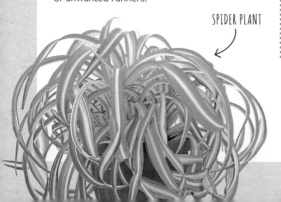

Fig trees come in a range of growth habits and leaf sizes.

Mosaic plant
Fittonia verschaffeltii
H1a, P, L, Bu
H&S 0.3m

This is a creeping, ground-cover plant noted for the coloured veins (usually white or pale pink) on its leaves. It is a good candidate for terrariums. Water regularly in summer, sparingly in winter. Feed in the summer. Prune only to remove dead stems.

Sensitive plant
Mimosa pudica
H1b, A/P, L, Bu
H 0.6m **S** 0.3m

The perennial sensitive plant can be treated as an annual. Its leaves naturally fold up and droop at night, and will also do so if touched (opening again after an hour or so). Fluffy, pom-pom-like flowers are borne in summer. Water regularly in summer, sparingly in winter. Feed in the summer. Prune only to remove dead stems.

Swiss cheese plant
Monstera deliciosa
H1b, P, L, Cl or **Tr**
H 4–8m **S** 2.5m

If given good conditions, Swiss cheese plants can reach triffid-like proportions. Even young plants have large leaves, showing the characteristic holes. The plant will be usually supplied with a moss-filled pole already in the pot to aid climbing. Water regularly in summer, sparingly in winter. Feed in the summer. Prune only to remove dead leaves and clean occasionally.

Sword fern
Nephrolepis exaltata
H1b, P, L, Fe
H&S 1m

This is a bushy plant that has the appearance one would expect from a fern. *N. exaltata* 'Bostoniensis' has more arching fronds, while 'Elegantissima' has thinner ones. Young plants can be borne on runners. Water regularly in summer, sparingly in winter. Feed in the summer. Prune only to remove dead fronds. Ensure the plant does not have permanently wet foliage, as this can cause the plant to rot.

Rock balsam
Peperomia
H1b, P, L, Bu
H&S 0.1–0.5m

A genus of over 1,000 species, which take many forms, the most suitable for growing in the house are those such as ivy leaf pepper (*P. griseoargentea*), which has silvery grey leaves, and emerald ripple (*P. caperata*). These both have heart-shaped, fleshy leaves, deeply veined, and bear rod-like flowers above the low-growing foliage. A collection of different-coloured varieties would make a good display. Water regularly in summer, sparingly in winter. Feed in the summer. Prune only to remove dead leaves and flower spikes.

MIMOSA

Swiss cheese plant climbs by hooking roots into a crevice (in the wild it would climb up a tree).

BRIGHT AND HUMID SPOTS

The following plants all need good light – but not direct sun – and high humidity, so a bathroom or kitchen windowsill would be a good choice for them. Boost the humidity, if needed, with regular misting sprays.

Tail flower
Anthurium andraeanum
H1a, P, F&L, Bu
H&S 0.5m

An unusual plant, with its waxy, tail-like flower, which is long-lasting and usually brightly coloured, supplemented with glossy, dark green, heart-shaped leaves. Flowers appear in spring and summer. Water regularly in summer but sparingly in winter. Mist as necessary to maintain high humidity. No pruning required; simply remove any dead leaves and flowers, and repot in fresh compost every other year.

Zebra plant
Goeppertia zebrina
H1a, P, L, Bu
H 1m **S** 0.5m

Formerly classified as *Calathea zebrina*, zebra plant has unsurprisingly stripy leaves in dark green and purple tones, which are red-purple on the underside. Water regularly in summer, sparingly in winter. Give a weak dilution of fertiliser in the summer. Prune only to cut out dead leaves.

Venus fly trap
Dionaea muscipula
H1c, P, L, Car, Bu
H 0.1m **S** 0.1m

A brilliant curiosity, but be aware that carnivorous plants are difficult to maintain. Refer to specialist websites and books for further care instructions. Keep compost moist and mist regularly to maintain very high humidity. Do not feed with fertiliser. Do not tempt the leaves to snap shut without a fly inside, as this will harm the plant.

Missionary plant
Pilea peperomioides
H1c, P, L, Bu
H&S 0.3m

Produces saucer-shaped leaves and, in summer, tiny pink/white flowers. The stem joins in the middle of the leaf on the underside. Leaves and stems can trail over the edge of the pot. Water regularly and feed monthly in summer. Prune to remove dead leaves and flowers.

Common staghorn fern
Platycerium bifurcatum
H1b, P, L, Fe
H&S 1m

An epiphyte, best grown in a mix of woodchip and moss, such as an orchid potting mix. It can be mounted on a wall, fixed to a piece of cork or similar, with sphagnum moss packed around the root ball. Prune only to remove dead leaves. Feed during the summer. In a pot, water freely in summer, sparingly in winter. For wall-mounted specimens, water by soaking the base and feed by adding fertiliser to the soaking water.

African violet
Saintpaulia
H1a, P, F, Bu
H 0.1m **S** 0.1m

A diminutive flowering house plant and ideal for small spaces. Flowers can last for months, and available colours range from deep purple-blue to pink to white. Although they require some humidity, misting can cause the leaves to rot. Water regularly in summer, sparingly in winter. Feed monthly in summer. Prune only to remove dead leaves and flowers.

The Venus fly trap is a useful if temperamental house plant.

AIR PLANTS

In the wild, air plants, such as *Tillandsia*, grow without soil and attach themselves to trees, rocks and other supports. Their dull-grey/greenish-blue foliage has no distinct leaves or stems, and is covered in tiny pores that allow them to absorb moisture and nutrients from the air. The various species of air plant – rosettes or stringy – lend themselves to being displayed in different ways, but they are at their most natural as hanging plants.

Place air plants in a spot with good ventilation in bright, but not direct, light. They will need a minimum temperature of 12°C and relatively high humidity. Water by plunging into tepid water (preferably rainwater or soft water)·two to three times a week (unless in high humidity, in which case allow to dry between watering). A specialist orchid fertiliser can be added monthly to the water (leave the air plant in the water for a few hours when feeding). Rosette-forming plants should be allowed to dry facing downwards so that water does not pool in the leaves. Prune only to remove dead leaves and flowers.

AIR PLANT

Air plants can
be housed in almost
anything — such
as these empty
seashells.

SHADY AND COOL SPOTS

There is a house plant for every room of the house, even a relatively dark and cold hallway or corridor. While it is still a good idea to keep plants out of very cold draughts, unheated rooms will suit these plants just fine. Bear in mind that shady does not mean complete darkness – every plant needs some light – but partial shade.

Plume asparagus
Asparagus densiflorus 'Myersii'
H1c, P, L, Fe
H&S 0.5m
Arching stems covered in thin, frond-like foliage and a few thorns. All parts of the plant are toxic if ingested. 'Myersii' is a more compact version of the straight species. Occasionally, small white flowers are followed by red berries. Water regularly in summer, sparingly in winter. Feed in the summer. Repot into fresh compost every other year – every year for young plants. Prune only to remove dead stems. To stimulate fresh growth, cut all stems back by half.

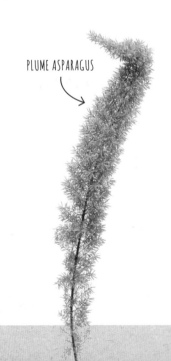

PLUME ASPARAGUS

Cast iron plant
Aspidistra elatior
H3, P, L, Bu
H 1m **S** 0.5m
Named because it is virtually impossible to kill, it is ideal for almost any position except full sun. Water regularly in summer (but avoid waterlogging), sparingly in winter. Feed in the summer. Prune only to remove dead leaves.

Hearts on a string
Ceropegia linearis subsp. *woodii*
H1c, P, L, Trai
H 1m **S** 0.1m
Borne intermittently on long, thin-trailing stems. Tubular pink flowers appear in summer. Grow in cactus compost (or a 50/50 mix of compost and grit). Water regularly in summer (but avoid waterlogging), sparingly in winter. Feed a diluted solution in the summer. Prune only to remove dead leaves and stems.

Persian cyclamen
Cyclamen persicum
H1c, P, F, Bu
H&S 0.2m
Heart-shaped leaves with silver markings and white, purple or pink flowers in winter and spring. When potting up, keep the tops of the tubers just above the soil surface. This plant can be liable to botrytis. All parts are toxic if ingested. Water and feed regularly when in growth (avoid splashing the leaves), sparingly when dormant. Once it has died back for the year, cut back dead flowers and all growth, or treat as a bulb (see page 136).

Cyclamen bring
colour to a
winter windowsill.

Castor oil plant
Ricinus communis
H5, P, L, Bu
H&S 4m

Although fully hardy, with its glossy palmate leaves, this makes a good house plant. Spikes of white flowers are borne in autumn. If restricted in a pot, it is unlikely to reach full size and can be pruned to further restrict its growth. Water regularly and feed in the summer (a dilute solution for smaller specimens). Prune only to remove dead stems and leaves or to restrict size.

Common ivy
Hedera helix
H5, P, L, Trai
H&S indefinite

Common ivy has many cultivars, some of which are variegated, but all will grow happily in almost full shade. They can be trimmed to fit any space and are easily trained. Water regularly and feed in the summer. Prune to remove dead parts and/or to restrict size.

Common passion flower
Passiflora caerulea
H4, P, F, Trai/Cl
H&S indefinite

Common passion flower's stunning flowers are wonderful to observe up close, but beware its ability to colonise a space. In spring, it can be cut back hard to a framework of main stems – try training it across an archway or window and allowing the side-shoots to hang downwards in a curtain. In good conditions, it may also bear edible fruits. Water regularly and feed in the summer (a dilute solution for smaller species). Prune only to remove dead stems and leaves or to restrict size.

Mind-your-own-business
Soleirolia soleirolii
H4, P, L, Bu/Trai
H 0.1m **S** indefinite

A ground-cover plant that can become invasive when outdoors, but will quickly fill a pot with a mat of low-growing, tiny green leaves. It could be used for a terrarium. Silver- and golden-leaved varieties are available. Water regularly. Feeding is not necessary. Trim back the foliage and roots as they exceed the boundaries of the pot.

PASSION FLOWER

Ivy makes a
great trailing house
plant for a
shady spot.

BULBS

Bulbs make rather good house plants, albeit temporary ones. When grown in a clear-glass container without soil, so that the developing roots can also be seen, they can also be a good way to get children interested in plants and gardening (the white roots on show also have a light, fresh appearance). Layering several bulbs between compost will mean a longer-lasting display, because the lowest bulbs will take longer to get to the surface and flower. For a maximum-impact display, single layers of bulbs can be packed in the pot so that there is hardly any compost visible.

Generally, bulbs are best used in a temporary indoor display and then planted out into the garden once they have finished flowering. In autumn, plant bulbs into a pot of multipurpose compost. Keep the pot moist, but not wet, and in a cold or cool place (ideally outside). Once the leaves start to show, keep in plenty of light. Bring into its display position once the flower buds have formed – the cooler this spot is, the longer the flowers will last. Keep well watered. Fertiliser is not necessary. Once all the flowers are finished (remove spent flowers if there are more still to come) plant the bulbs in the garden or dispose in the compost heap.

Amaryllis
Hippeastrum
A classic bulb, planted alone in a pot, and bought for Christmas displays. Usually red or white flowers, sometimes with several per stem. Leaves appear after the flower spike.

Hyacinth
Hyacinthus
A couple of these flowers will be sufficient to scent an entire room. Available in a range of colours and shades. Traditionally, the hyacinth are bought as forced bulbs for indoor display.

Daffodil
Narcissus
Specific daffodil varieties have been developed that are ideal for either forcing (such as 'Paper White') or small pots ('Tête-à tête').

Crocus
Crocus
The honeyed fragrance is best appreciated up close, and so a pot or two of these small flowers is worth growing. It is even possible to cultivate saffron in a pot, using *Crocus sativus* bulbs.

Snowdrop
Galanthus
Minute variations of green patterns can appear on a snowdrop petal, but even the most basic form, *G. nivalis*, brings a welcome sign of spring.

Tulip
Tulipa
The simple form of the tulip flower works both in isolation (a forced bulb in a single vase) and in a group. Dwarf forms are available for small spaces, but many of the varieties will not flower again the following year.

Mix different
bulbs in assorted
containers for a
springtime display.

GLOSSARY

Akadama The clay-like soil used for bonsai and kokedama planting.

Annual A plant that completes its life cycle within a year, growing from seeds to flowering and then dying off.

Bare-root plant A plant supplied in a bag, not a pot of compost.

Biennial A plant that puts on foliage in the first year of growth, overwinters and then flowers and dies in the second year.

Botrytis (*Botrytis cinerea*) A grey mould typically infecting plants that are damaged or in humid situations.

Capillary matting A carpet-like material that is used under pots, through which water can be drawn up like a wick.

Crocks Pieces of broken pot traditionally used to aid drainage when placed in the base of the pot.

Cutting A small piece of stem and leaves removed from the plant and potted in order that it will produce roots and grow into a new plant. Plants multiplied in this way will be genetically identical.

Dormant When a plant stops growing (e.g. over winter) but does not die. Also refers to the means of the seed surviving over a (long) time so that it will not germinate until conditions are favourable.

Drip-line irrigation A system, either home-made or bought, that distributes water between a number of pots or hanging containers by dripping slowly and, usually, continuously.

Epiphytes Plants that use other plants or rocks for support but do not parasitise them (e.g. orchids).

Forcing Bringing plants into fruit or flower earlier than they would naturally by manipulating the environment.

Hydroponics A system of growing plants in a stream of water and soluble nutrients rather than soil or compost, typically utilised for green walls.

Kokedama The Japanese art of displaying plants in mud and moss balls rather than pots.

Macramé A style of craft made from knotted string, popular in the 1970s.

Microclimate A small area with its own particular variations in temperature, wind, light and humidity levels.

Misting Spraying plants with a fine mist of water to increase humidity in the air.

Orchid pot A clear plastic or glass pot particularly used for growing plants with roots that use sunlight for photosynthesis.

Perennial A plant that grows year on year (as opposed to an annual).

Perlite A material, formed of tiny white balls, used to aid drainage in compost.

Photosynthesis The process by which plants create their own food using sunlight, water and carbon dioxide.

Phototropism The process by which plants grow towards the strongest light source.

Pot-bound A plant whose roots have taken up all the space in the pot, leaving no room for further growth and little compost.

Potting on Transplanting seedlings or young plants into bigger pots to give them room to keep growing.

Potting up Moving a seedling or bare-root plant into a container, or putting a plant into a new but similarly sized pot.

Repotting The process of transferring a plant grown in a container into a new pot the same size, after reducing the root ball slightly to make room for fresh compost.

Rock wool A plant growth material typically used in place of compost in hydroponic systems.

Root ball The roots of the plant and the compost or soil that surrounds them once they are removed from the pot or ground.

Sphagnum moss A type of moss that is used for decoration or as a growing medium.

Substrate The material, such as compost or perlite, in or on which a plant anchors its roots in a hydroponic system.

Terrarium A glass vessel which contains plants that can be sealed so the plants form an ecosystem within the container.

Tying in Using string or wire to fix wayward stems of climbing or trailing plants to their supports.

Underplant Planting low-growing plants under taller specimens to mimic nature and make best use of space.

FURTHER RESOURCES

The RHS website has a wealth of information about growing and caring for plants, as well as the Plant Finder search tool and general gardening advice. RHS members can also use the Advisory Service:
www.rhs.org.uk

Many specialist nurseries have plant care information on their websites. Some plant groups also have societies dedicated to promoting the attractions of those plants, such as succulents, and these websites can be good sources of information.

Plant and equipment sources:
Architectural Plants
www.architecturalplants.com

Dibleys Nurseries
www.dibleys.com

Etsy
www.etsy.com

House of Plants
www.houseofplants.co.uk

London Terrariums
www.londonterrariums.com

Not on the High Street
www.notonthehighstreet.com

For DIY hydroponic growing kits and information:
IKEA
www.ikea.com

Seed Pantry
www.seedpantry.co.uk

Home Hydro Systems
www.homehydrosystems.com

Ditch the Dirt: How to grow beautiful, edible, hydroponic plants at home by Rob Laing (Dovetail March 2018)

Books for further information and ideas:
RHS Pests and Diseases by Andrew Halstead and Pippa Greenwood (RHS/ Dorling Kindersley 2009)

RHS Grow Your Own: Crops in Pots by Kay Maguire (RHS/Mitchell Beazley 2013)

RHS Miniature Garden Grower by Holly Farrell ((RHS/Mitchell Beazley 2016)

RHS Plants from Pips by Holly Farrell (RHS/Mitchell Beazley 2015)

RHS Gardening for Mindfulness by Holly Farrell (RHS/Mitchell Beazley 2017)

INDEX

A

African violet 65, 128
agave 78, 112
air plants 65, 130–131
aloe 57, 78, 112
amaryllis 55, 136
annuals 28
Arabian coffee 118
auriculas 65

B

bamboo palm 73
bamboo plant 73
banner plant 58
Barberton daisy 73
basil 61, 66, 110
bathrooms 48–51
bay 53
Benjamin tree 73
bird of paradise 121
bird's nest fern 116, 119
borage 66
Boston fern 65, 73
bougainvillea 106
bromeliads 65
bulbs 40, 55, 75, 136–137

C

cacti 57, 65, 112
Cape primrose 65, 121
care 84–99
cast iron plant 132
castor oil plant 134
chamomile 61
children 18, 56–59
chilli pepper 70, 106
Chinese evergreen 73
Christmas cactus 115
Christmas displays 52–55

cigar plant 28, 108
citrus 65, 108
cleaning 90–91
climbing plants 32–33, 95
cocktail gardens 66–67
coleus 110
compost 27, 29, 37
conifers 52, 53
containers 19, 24–25, 26
coriander 61, 110
creeping fig 37
crimson bottlebrush 106
crocus 136
croton 58, 124
ctenanthe 58
cucamelons 61, 66
cucumbers 61, 66, 70
cymbidium 122

D

daffodil 55, 75, 136
damage 101
dampness 15
delta maidenhair fern 65, 124
desk displays 72–73
diseases 98–99
displaying plants 16–19
drainage 25, 31
dwarf fan palm 116
dwarf mountain palm 116
dwarf pomegranate 108

E

echeveria 45, 78, 115
edible planting 60–63, 66–71
equipment 26–27
evergreens 52

F

feeding 88–89, 100
flat palm 118
forced bulbs 55
four-leaved pink sorrel 118
fruits 60

G

ginger roots 67, 80
grape hyacinth 75

H

hanging gardens 19, 48–51
hearts on string 50, 132
herbs 60, 70
holiday care 92–93
houseleeks 45
humidity 15, 87, 93, 128–131
hyacinth 136
hydroponic systems 68–71

I

iris 75
ivy 50, 53, 73, 134, 135

J

jasmine 65

K

kalanchoe 115
kitchens 18, 60–63, 66–67
kokedama 40–43

L

leaf scorch 101
lemon balm 61
lemon basil 66
lemon grass 65
lemon thyme 66

lemon verbena 65, 66
lettuce 70
lilies 65
lily turf 73
living stones 57, 115
location 13, 14, 85, 116–121, 128–135

M

Madagascar dragon tree 17, 73, 118
mibuna 70
microclimates 12–13
mind-your-own-business 134
mindfulness 64–65
miniature date palm 73
mint 61, 67
missionary plant 129
misting 87
mizuna 70
money tree 57, 115
mosaic plant 126
moth orchid 122
Mother-in-law's tongue 120, 121

N

nasturtiums 61
natal lily 118, 119
nutrient deficiency 100

O

olive 53
orchids 25, 122–123
ornamental fig 58, 124, 125

P

parsley 61, 110
passion flower 134
peace lily 121
pebble plant 115

pelargonium 65, 66, 80–81, 108
peppers 70
perennials 28
Persian cyclamen 132
pests 96–97
photosynthesis 84–85
phototropsim 15
pineapple 116
plume asparagus 132
pollutants 72
pot-bound plants 101
pot marigolds 28
pot mum 73
pots 19, 24–25, 26
potting 30
propogation 78–81
pruning 94–95

Q

quarantine 23

R

radishes 61
repotting 30–31, 101
rock balsam 126
rocket 70
root pruning 94
rose-scented pelargonium 66
rosemary 53, 61, 110

S

sage 61
salad leaves 61, 68–69, 70
seasonal displays 18, 52–55, 74–77
seeds, sowing 28–29
sensitive plant 126
sensory gardens 56–59
shaping plants 94
snowdrops 40, 75, 136

sourcing plants 22–23
spider plant 50, 73, 79, 124
spring displays 74–77
spring onions 61
staghorn fern 128
strawberries 61, 66
string gardens 40–43
succulents 23, 44–47, 56, 78, 112–115
supporting plants 32–33
Swiss cheese plant 33, 126, 127
sword fern 126

T

tail flower 73, 128
temperature variations 14, 15
terrariums 36–39
texture 58
thyme 61, 66, 110
tomatoes 61, 70
tools 26–27
trailing plants 50, 61, 95
tropical hibiscus 108
tulips 136

V

vanda 122
vegetables 60
Venus fly trap 128, 129

W

walls 60, 68
watering 86–87, 93, 100
wheatgrass 70
windowsills 14–15, 66–67
workspaces 72–73

Z

zebra plant 128

CREDITS